More Praise for *Wayne*

"Each day three children in the United States die from child abuse in the home. It's one of the most urgent problems facing our nation. For more than twenty years, I've worked to raise public awareness of the child abuse crisis and to encourage people to become part of the solution. Wayne Theodore's painful, courageous, and moving account of his life story vividly shows how vital it is for all of us to do what we can to help prevent child abuse."

—Cheryl Ladd
Celebrity Ambassador, Childhelp USA®

"Wayne gives you a unique opportunity to see the world through the eyes of a victim of child abuse. You'll feel his wounds and you'll share his inner courage as he somehow finds the strength to triumph over pain and degradation. It's impossible to read this book and come away unchanged."

—Marilyn Van Derbur
Former Miss America and child abuse survivor

"Wayne Theodore gives a powerful voice to millions of tragically abused children who are scared silent by their abusers. His family's horrendous story is a mixture of denial, enabling, fear, the struggle to heal and the inspiring power of the will to survive. It also demonstrates the almost unconscious manner in which an abused child can easily and unwittingly become an abuser to the next generation. That's why the work of Childhelp USA®—helping to break the cycle of abuse—is so important."

—Sara O'Meara
Co-Founder and Chairman, Childhelp USA®

"This brutally honest telling of Wayne Theodore's life story shows how the tragic scars of child abuse can last a lifetime. Unfortunately, experiences like Wayne's are not anomalies. His story underscores the fact that all of us MUST do what we can to help prevent child abuse in our communities."

—A. Sidney Johnson III
President and CEO
Prevent Child Abuse America

"A courageous and powerful story of one man's determination to break the cycle of repeat abuse, Wayne dramatizes the importance of American Humane's mission to prevent cruelty, abuse and neglect of all children and animals."

—Timothy M. O'Brien
President, American Humane

"Wayne's eye-opening story tells it like it is—the suffering; the betrayal of those who could have helped, but chose instead to look the other way; and the ongoing challenges of healing abuse. This personal story of courage and perseverance pleads with each of us to work for justice and the healing of all children whose cries have not been heard. Perhaps, this is the greatest inspiration of Wayne's story—that we who read it are prompted to act for the protection and safety of all children."

—Dawn Beye, MSW, LCSW
Executive Director
Child Abuse Prevention Association

Wayne

AN ABUSED CHILD'S STORY
OF COURAGE, SURVIVAL, AND HOPE

Wayne

AN ABUSED CHILD'S STORY OF COURAGE, SURVIVAL, AND HOPE

Wayne Theodore
with Leslie Alan Horvitz

HARBOR PRESS
GIG HARBOR, WASHINGTON

Library of Congress Cataloging-in-Publication Data

Wayne Theodore, 1958–
    Wayne: an abused child's story of courage, survival, and hope/Wayne
Theodore with Leslie A. Horvitz.
        p. cm.
    ISBN 0-936197-45-5 (alk. paper)
    1. Wayne Theodore, 1958– 2. Adult child abuse victims—United
States—Biography. 2. Abused children—United States—Biography.
I. Horvitz, Leslie A., 1948– II. Title.

HV6626.52 .W39 A3 2003
362.76(092—dc21
[B]

                                                            2002032925

Publisher's Note: This is a work of non-fiction. However, all individuals mentioned in the book have been given pseudonyms with the exception of the author and various public figures, whose actual names are used. The author's parents and siblings, who have previously appeared on national television to discuss some of the incidents that are described in the book, have been given pseudonymous first names.

WAYNE: An Abused Child's Story of Courage, Survival, and Hope

Book design and composition by RohaniDesign.com.

Printed in the United States of America
10 9 8 7 6 5 4 3 2 1

Harbor Press, Inc.
P.O. Box 1656
Gig Harbor, WA 98335

www.harborpress.com

CONTENTS

FOREWORD

In my years in front of the camera, I have had many unforgettable moments. Every day I meet people who have faced enormous tragedy, personal misfortune, and the loss of mind, body, and spirit. But the memory of one show about one family and the courage of one man has never left me. That man is Wayne Theodore, and the show is the one that presented his story. It deeply affected everyone who ever saw it, and it is still the show I am asked about most. Wayne's survival without having been given even the most basic tools of humanity is simply a miracle.

In reviewing Wayne's book, I revisited the details of that particular show once again in my mind and I remembered so clearly this powerful story. During the show, I witnessed members of this family recall their abuse and then confront their abuser with questions that had lain hidden until the camera began rolling. As Freud said, "The only way to forget is to remember," and remembering in this way was one of the first steps for Wayne in his long struggle to heal from the years of abuse he suffered.

Wayne knew the power of television and he understood its potential impact. When good television tackles a serious subject such as child abuse, it can change us forever, making us more sensitive to the possibilities life holds and more aware of the harsh realities, as well. We can reach out to a society that needs and wants to be educated by openly examining real issues with sympathy, candor, and care. As Wayne and his siblings shared their stories of unthinkable physical and emotional abuse, you could clearly see the profound effect it had on the audience. This is one of the most valuable contributions of the television talk show format and the aspect of the show that I, personally, find most rewarding.

Overcoming intense fear and extreme repression, and learning how to love and accept, make Wayne's story a true inspiration for all of us. Wayne's struggle and ultimate triumph over a childhood filled with pain and degradation will renew your faith in the extraordinary power and strength of the human spirit. I am proud to have had the opportunity to present his story on my show and make the public aware of this remarkable man.

—SALLY JESSY RAPHAEL
NEW YORK, NEW YORK

ACKNOWLEDGMENTS

I would like to thank all of the people who contributed to this project: Harry Lynn, the publisher at Harbor Press, who believed in this book and enthusiastically gave me the support I needed to tell my story. Leslie Horvitz, a great listener and an even better writer for helping me put my words onto paper, and for his sensitive and careful approach to this book. Debby Young, my editor, for her talent, perceptiveness, and ability to read between the lines. Her honesty and integrity made it easy for us to develop the kind of trusting and open relationship that added so much to the creation of this book. Jean Tang, a talented writer who helped out with portions of the book. Sally Jessy Raphael, for giving me the first opportunity to tell my story at a very crucial time in my life.

Most importantly, I would like to thank God and my family for giving me the strength and ability to survive and to create this life that I love.

The Theodore Family

Carl and Ruth, parents

Joseph, b. 1955

Susan, b. 1957

John, b. 1957

Wayne, b. 1958

Michael, b. 1959

Christopher, b. 1961

Sheila, b. 1962

Gail, b. 1964

Brian, b. 1966

Kenny, b. 1968

Gary, b. 1972

Linda, b. 1973

PROLOGUE

Summer is a peaceful time in New Hampshire. In May, after the rainy season, most of it is covered with a nice thick blanket of green. Just standing outside doing nothing in the middle of a field, you can smell berries, new leaves, honeysuckle, and fresh-cut grass. It's a good healthy smell—pure nature.

When I smell this for the first time every year, I stop thinking about all the things on my to-do list, like how to approach a new work project, or what color to paint the two-story barn we just built, or whether the girls' varsity softball team that I coach is going to win against the home team this weekend. When I smell this smell, all of that disappears. Instead, for a moment, I think about how gorgeous life is.

My wife Sharon and I live with our four daughters, aged six through sixteen, on a New Hampshire farm. It's not big—only nine acres—and instead of chickens and crops, we have horses and cows. They're not for breeding, milking, or selling; they're just for fun. My daughters ride the horses and I raise two bulls and a heifer—as pets. Because I'm not a farmer, I like to think of it as a "gentleman's farm." I'm a contractor. I build roads for new subdivisions and put in sewer lines. I've done okay with it, and although we're not a multimillion-dollar company, I usually give out Christmas bonuses so the men who work for me can buy their families something special.

This is my life—peaceful and comfortable. I don't know what's going to happen tomorrow. Who does? But for the time being, I have my family and a solid business. It works, and I'm happy.

Still, my childhood—the terrifying and shocking way I grew up—is never far from my mind. The horror of it is always there, biding its time, waiting to hit me when I least expect it.

It's usually something that, to everyone else, seems like nothing—broken glass on the floor, or a little mold on a piece of bread, or a car driving slowly up a gravel road. For me, though, these are major triggers. When I see broken glass, my first reaction—my gut instinct—is to run and hide. When I see mold on bread, I feel embarrassed, like I'm naked at school and everyone's pointing at me, laughing. When I hear tires roll along gravel, it makes my chest feel hollow—like a cut-up tree trunk left in the woods to rot, and in the hollow a fear runs so deep that I have to sit on my hands for a moment to keep them from shaking.

The past has a habit of coming to the surface at the strangest times—good times, as well as bad times. Like when my daughter Amy won a first-prize ribbon in an A-rated horse show, the most competitive kind. She was only fourteen then, a freshman in high school, and she'd beat out adults, people who live and breathe horses and don't have to work hard—like she does—to get on the honor roll. She walked into the arena, this cocky little fourteen-year-old girl with her blue eyes and blonde ponytail, and no one ever would have guessed that this was her first A-rated show. When I saw her I thought, *that's me—that was me when I was fourteen.* Confident, daring, downright bratty. Then I had to correct myself. *That's the me I would have been, or could have been, if I'd been given half a chance.*

There's a movie projector in my head that keeps showing the same black-and-white reruns. The pictures are of my family—the one I grew up in—and a farm. It's not the farm I live on now with my wife and daughters; it's another one, and it's nowhere near as peaceful. The farm where I grew up was wild, and my memories of it have nothing to do with gentlemen, or hobbies, or the incredible beauty of family love.

I'm Wayne Theodore, and I was an abused child. I'm forty-four this year, and I can finally say this without choking on the words. I can say it without having to duck my head down into a bottomless ocean of shame.

I grew up in a family of twelve kids, with a mother who disappeared as often as she was pregnant, and a psychotic father who had twisted ideas about how to keep her—and us kids—in line. I grew up in an island fortress, eating food not fit for human consumption, with siblings who spied on each other to save their own skins and maybe to get a decent meal.

When you're an abused child, your life is a secret. You stay home from school if you have new injuries people can see. You cover for the abuser, and you lie to anyone who asks questions. You make few friends. You tell no one. You trust nothing. *You believe you're worthless.*

But you don't have to believe that forever—and you don't have to live with the shame and the secrecy forever. It's not easy, but you can make a new life for yourself if you have the determination and the will to start over. It takes courage to look at your past head-on, and then to try to move beyond it. And it takes time—but it can be done. For me, it was worth all the pain and struggle it took.

I knew what I had to do if I wanted to put the past behind me and make a decent life for myself and my family, so I set out on the most important journey of my life.

This is my story.

When I was six years old my father almost killed me. It was a bitterly cold day in early February. My brother John and I shared a bunk bed that was jammed up against a wall. The top bunk, where I slept, was next to a window. I couldn't see out, though, because the window was always covered in plastic. One night, when I turned over, I swung my foot out and put it through the pane. I must have been sleeping pretty soundly, because this didn't wake me up. When I opened my eyes a few hours later I had a feeling something was wrong, but I didn't know what it was until I saw the broken glass strewn over the blanket. At first I didn't understand what the broken glass was doing there. Then I glanced at the window, saw a jagged hole, and realized what I'd done. I'd also wet the bed.

I lay there, guilty and terrified, desperately trying to figure out what to do. I peered down to the lower bunk, but no one was there. John must have been getting ready for school. I couldn't hear a sound. It was nearly eight-thirty. Had I overslept? Maybe my father had already left for work. That would mean I'd be spared a beating—at least until he got home.

Then I heard him. My father has a gravelly voice—real deep—and on that morning it was hoarse and he was yelling at my mother. He was in a bad mood; it sounded worse than usual. He must have been out drinking, I thought; maybe he'd overslept and woken up with a hangover. He was usually gone by eight-thirty. My heart sank. Only a miracle would save me now.

The wait was agony. I was paralyzed, already tensing against the blows I knew would come. After a few minutes I heard my father's heavy footsteps approaching my room. I closed my eyes, pretending to sleep—a gut reaction. He walked into the bedroom. For a moment nothing happened, but I could feel his presence. I could hear—and feel—his hot breath on my shoulder. Then it came.

"What the hell?" he yelled, in that gravelly voice. He reached his hands out—big, beefy hands—and yanked me up off the bed by my hair. "What did you do, you little son of a bitch? You broke the window, didn't you?" Before I could answer him he flung me down to the floor, head first. Then he punched me and kicked me, and punched and kicked some more. I just lay there, my small body still, trying hard not to cry out. Then he stopped. I don't know why; maybe he was so hungover that he didn't have the energy for it.

"I'll finish you off later, you little bastard," he muttered.

It's hard to say where I hurt the most. When I moved my legs, it hurt. When I put my hands on my face, it hurt. When I stayed still, it hurt.

I wished as hard as I could that he would go off to work and leave me alone. Now I had to stay home because my teacher would notice the bruises on my face.

When nothing else happened, I thought I'd be okay for the rest of the day: I'd already gotten my morning beating. I didn't consider this unfair, either; I thought I deserved it. Hadn't I done something wrong by breaking the window and wetting the bed?

I dressed slowly and carefully to avoid touching my swollen, bruised body, and then I went to the kitchen. My mother sat at one end of the table, my father at the other, and I took a place between them. The sun streamed through the window. No one said a word.

My father's face was pale and his eyes were bloodshot. He was glaring at me, but he said nothing. I could tell he was still steamed up about the window and the wet mattress. My mother, meanwhile, pretended that nothing was going on.

Although my father had finished eating, he stayed at the table, just looking at me as if he were sizing me up. He muttered under his breath—"You little shit, you little shit"—working himself up. My mother was humming, just sort of singing to herself, which was her way of shutting out unpleasantness. I just sat there, barely able to swallow. Breakfast was the usual—moldy bread and peanut butter. Half the time

I wasn't sure whether I was biting down on the bread or my own sore and swollen lips. I tried not to look at my father; I didn't want to antagonize him further. But I didn't know where else to look. I kept hoping he'd leave for work—he was already an hour late—so I'd be let off the hook. But I had a feeling he wasn't finished with me.

Suddenly he lunged up from the table and grabbed me by the hair. He punched me until I sank to the floor. Blood gushed out of my nose and mouth—so much blood I couldn't tell where it was coming from. He dragged me into the bathroom, and then he threw me face-down on the floor next to the tub and held my hands in a vise-like grip behind my back.

I was six years old, and I couldn't remember when the beatings had started. But I was sure my father had never done anything like this before. I didn't know what to expect. With his free hand he turned on the taps—all the way. We had no stopper, so he stuffed a rag into the drain.

He began to pound my head against the side of the tub, again and again. My nose was so swollen and stuffed up that I couldn't breathe and I was gagging because of all the blood that was seeping down my throat. As soon as I saw him getting ready to hammer me I tightened my skin so it wouldn't hurt as much. I was ready for the punches in the head and punches in the back. The only thing I couldn't protect was my hair. This time, though, he hit me in places where he'd never hit me before, like the back of my legs, so I couldn't tighten my skin in time.

I wanted to cry out *Don't! Please! Help me!* Hadn't he punished me enough? But the impact was too powerful, and I struggled just to keep breathing through the blood and the pain. I knew I was bad, I deserved my beating, but I didn't do it on purpose. Why couldn't he stop?

But he didn't stop. I wondered whether he ever would.

I listened to the sound of water rushing into the tub.

All of a sudden, he lifted me off the floor by my arms and threw me into the tub, face down.

Even before I felt the water swirling around my head I saw it turning red. It took me a few moments to realize that it was from my blood. I'm bleeding badly, I thought. The tub was full of what had been inside of me just a few seconds ago. I took in a big gulp of blood and water. I was gagging and choking. It wasn't that I hurt—the pain wasn't killing me yet—it was that I didn't know what was going to happen, how much of my blood my father wanted to take.

He held my legs in the air to keep me under. I tried to push myself out enough to get my head above water, but I just couldn't. My small body wasn't strong enough, and I didn't have anything to grab onto. I struggled not to inhale but water was seeping into my nostrils. I felt panic coming on, and I knew that soon I wouldn't be able to keep my lips clenched shut, and then I would start swallowing water—and that would be it.

Finally, he relaxed his grip a little. I pushed up my head so I could get a little air. Maybe he'll stop now, I thought; maybe he's decided that he's taught me a lesson, and he'll let me go. Then I saw my mother sitting in a chair just outside the open bathroom door; she was watching what was going on. She wore a big gray dress that came down to her knees. She said something to my father but I couldn't hear what it was. Then, before I knew what was happening, my father jammed my head back under the water. I took in a big gulp because I hadn't been ready. As bad as the beatings were before, they were never like this. I was scared out of my mind. I was ready to give up. *Please,* I wanted to say. *I'll do whatever you want me to. I'll be a good boy. Just let me go.*

When my father let me up again, I saw that my mother hadn't moved. She was very calm, and she wouldn't look at me. She was staring off into space. *Ma, why won't you look at me?*

This time when she spoke to my father I heard every word. "Carl," she said, "please stop. You're going to kill him."

You're going to kill him.

I knew she was right. This time he meant it; this time he *was* going to kill me. Now I looked at her, hoping she'd rescue me, but her face was blank. There was nothing in her eyes. She didn't move. I realized with a sinking heart that my mother wasn't going to get out of the chair. *She's not going to do anything to stop him. She can't help me. Not because she doesn't want to, but because she simply can't. She's as powerless as I am. I'm alone. I'm alone with him.* There was no one else in that house who might come and save me. At least when my brothers and sisters were around I had some protection. They could watch what he was doing. He'd only go so far if he knew people were watching. This time he had no witnesses.

There was no one to help me. No one. And this time he wasn't going to stop. This beating was different. This time I couldn't protect myself. There was burning hatred in this beating. This wasn't just punishment. This was murder. *I'm going to die.*

My heart was racing so fast that I was sure it was going to burst through my skin. But then something happened.

The pain went away. It was as if the beating were happening to somebody else, another little kid. It was me, but not me *exactly*. It felt like I suddenly disappeared from myself, like a safety hatch had opened up and sucked me in. I was there, and then suddenly I wasn't. My father kept beating me, but I didn't feel it anymore.

At the moment this happened, everything slowed down, and then froze, like somebody snapping a photo in slow motion. My father's fist hovered in midair; his face was red with rage; his eyes were glazed and unseeing. My mother sat in the chair, her mouth open wide as if she were about to scream. And I was in the tub, in water so bloody you could hardly see through it. But there was no sound. It was as if I floated above this scene.

Then time began to move forward again and my father went back to beating me—but I was very calm, because I was somewhere else. This beating was happening to some other little boy; I had buried myself in a safe place where he couldn't reach me. It was like pulling the bedcovers over me, but these covers made me invisible. Somehow I knew my father could pound me all he wanted and it would have no effect. His fists seemed to pass right through me, as if I were made of air.

I had this strange feeling that I would survive as long as I could stay in my safe place. I would be protected there. I was strong and powerful there. While I hid in my safe place, he was beating someone who didn't even exist. I knew that if I poked out my head he'd get me again, and I'd be dead.

I don't know how long the beating lasted. I lost all track of time. Then something changed in him. It was like a bell went off in his head. Maybe he realized it was getting late, and that he'd better go to work. But maybe, I thought, maybe he knew about my new power, that he knew I'd found a place beyond him. I hoped so.

Whatever the truth was, at that moment he sagged, as if all the fight had gone out of him. He let go of me. "Get out!" he screamed.

I was grateful it was over, but for a few moments I couldn't do anything. When I finally managed to climb out of the tub, my knees were so weak I just sort of collapsed and lay motionless, crunched up on the floor. I knew he wasn't quite through with me. He'd want to get in a few more kicks and smacks.

"I'm coming back after you when I get home from work," he warned.

I still didn't dare move. I feared he might try to drown me again. But instead he just turned to my mother and said, "Ruth, if he leaves the yard today be sure and let me know. He isn't to leave the yard!"

With that, he stormed out of the bathroom.

But he'd be back. I knew the torture wasn't over, but something had changed.

Without saying anything, my mother got down on her hands and knees in the bathroom and began cleaning up the blood with some rags. She was nervous and droopy, and she wouldn't look me in the eye. For a while I wondered whether she was even aware that I was still there. Then she reached out and handed me a wet rag to hold on my nose. I took it, but the blood kept pouring out, anyway. When she'd finished wiping the floor, she swished the water in the tub to rinse the blood off the sides and let the water out.

Then I heard his footsteps: He was coming back after me. Maybe he really was going to kill me. Then my father left the house, slamming the door behind him. He hadn't come back for me, after all.

My mother picked up the bloody rags and walked out of the bathroom. I expected her to say, "Wayne, go and get dressed now," or something like that, but she never said a word. She just left me there curled up on the bathroom floor, like I was something she'd forgotten to clean up.

I was dizzy and sick from the beating. I wasn't supposed to be in the bathroom, and if he came home and found me still there, I'd get beaten for that, too. But I needed—right that second—to see what I looked like.

I climbed onto the counter next to the sink to look into the mirror. What I saw stopped me dead.

As a boy, I had light blond hair. My father kept all us boys in crew cuts, so I had one even at that age. I think my features have always been pretty tough—wide-set hazel eyes that can stare you down, a wide forehead, a squarish jaw, a strong nose, with a crease—not a dimple—running down each cheek. That day I didn't recognize my own face.

My nose, which had been broken, was the bloody centerpiece. If you looked closely through the mess of blood and mucous, the tip of it was squashed somewhere off to the side, separate from the bone. I could see a little cartilage—a glimpse of white. My eyes were moist and shining, but you had to look hard to see them: Both upper and lower lids were badly bruised, and my upper cheeks were swelling into two big balloons. I discovered, to my surprise, I'd been crying, so my tears were running together with the blood from cuts across my forehead. I just stared at my face—soaking wet, battered and swollen, with my broken nose bent out of shape. Tears were streaming down my face.

That's you, I whispered. I wanted to be sure to remember what I looked like. I wanted to brand my brain with the image—like I'd seen cows and horses get branded. My father beat me all the time, but this had been far worse than anything before, and I wasn't going to let myself forget it.

I also wanted to remember the feeling I had of being in another person's body. That could come in handy. It was like I'd come back from faraway, from another planet, to see this little boy—damaged and trembling in terror. I wanted to tell the boy in the mirror that he shouldn't be so afraid. He'd survived this time, and he'd survive again.

I told myself I was made out of metal. My father beat me up today and every other day, but I wasn't *beaten.* And one more thing: Someday I'd fight back.

My first idea was to beat him up or do something else to hurt him physically. But how could I hurt him when I was so little? No, I'd have to get a lot bigger and stronger before I could take him.

Then I had another idea. *I'm going to tell on him.* That was a big, big thing. That was much bigger than beating him up. *Someday I'm going to tell on him.* I'd let the world know what he did. That was my mission. That was what I had to grow up and do. I couldn't count on my brothers and sisters to do it; they'd cave in to him too easily. This was my responsibility. I had to grow up and tell on him.

But if I was going to grow up, I had to stay alive. And to do that I had to remember how to get back to that safe place where my father could never find me. So I made a pact with myself: if I was true to my mission, then nothing could ever happen to me. My father could beat me from morning 'til night, but if I could get to that hiding place where I had the power, where I was invisible, then he couldn't really touch me.

The past began to open up in the most ordinary way—with a phone call from my "little" brother Brian. He's eight years younger than I am. At the time of this call I was in my early thirties, so Brian was a grown man.

Brian and I talked all the time, but when he called me that winter morning his voice sounded strained. He was depressed, more depressed than I'd remembered him ever being before. Brian was having some personal problems, and he'd hit rock bottom trying to figure them all out.

We talked for a while, and I tried to give him some advice—the usual stuff, like what I would do if I were in his shoes, and to cheer up, that everything would work itself out eventually. But we'd had this conversation before, and this time Brian wasn't satisfied with it—he needed something else, something that took me completely by surprise.

"You're smart, Wayne," he blurted, "probably smarter than the rest of us." He meant the family—all our brothers and sisters. I waited for more; there was silence while Brian fished around for the right words. Finally, he said, "I've got to ask you something, Wayne. I have a feeling you'd know."

"Know what, Brian?"

"I don't know why I act the way I do, why I do the things I do." Then he said, almost in a whisper, "I don't want to be violent, like Dad."

Brian went on. "This stuff keeps happening to me—you know what I mean—and it happens to all of us, all the time, over and over again. It's our lives, Wayne, and you could help me—you could help us. You're the one who really knows most about this situation with our lives."

He didn't have to say any more. I knew exactly what he was talking about. "Brian, I'll do whatever I can to help you."

And I had every intention of keeping my promise.

There was a lot I didn't remember, or want to remember. Still, I knew, better than younger Brian, that our parents had treated us badly; it was a relief to be able to talk about it. I used to make excuses for my bad behavior, always blaming the other guy, assuming that everybody was out to get me. Then it would hit me: *Why did I do that? Why can't I stop the anger, the violent behavior?*

So when my brother asked me those questions, it really hit home.

I wasn't alone. I could begin to talk about some of the stuff that had been bottled up inside of me my whole life. I felt exactly the way Brian did. The abuse had warped all of us.

It made me feel good to open up. After all this time, I finally had something like an ally. It's one thing to be in a bad place by yourself, but when there's someone to share that place with you, it's not so shameful. We talked about things that had built up in silence for years and years. I'd gone through a lot more than Brian had, because I was one of the first six kids, and while the younger kids had suffered a lot, none of them had gone through what I had. For whatever reason, I was beaten harder and more often than any of my siblings. But it didn't matter, not then: We'd both been violated, both cheated out of our childhoods—and we were both in some form of denial about it.

Even as I was saying this I knew it wasn't the whole story. "Our parents did a lot to us that we still don't know about," I said.

"What do you mean, our 'parents'?" Brian said. "Ma was a victim, too."

"Then why did she sit there and do nothing when we were getting beaten? Why did she go off and leave us with him all those times? Why did she do that if she was so concerned about us?" I thought about what my wife would have done in a similar situation. "Look at Sharon," I said. "Look at my beautiful babies. I could never hurt my babies in a million years, much less abandon them. If I ever hurt one of my babies, if I ever so much as laid a hand on them, my wife would either leave with the kids or throw me out. Or have me arrested."

Brian listened to what I was saying, but I could tell he wasn't buying it, not completely.

"Look, Brian," I said, "there's no way you can tell me that Ma's not somewhat to blame."

"You're crazy. Poor innocent Ma? There's absolutely no way she's involved in any of what happened." By this time, my parents were divorced and Ma had remarried and moved to Arizona.

"Okay, Brian, let me call her up and I'll put it to her. I'll ask her why she abandoned us and see what she has to say."

Brian didn't believe I'd find out anything more than I had in the past. He had a point. I'd tried to put the pieces together before, and she'd just clammed up.

"I know every time I talk to Ma she just runs and hides," I said. "She won't even acknowledge my questions. But we all have a right to know, and this time I'm not going to stop until I get a straight answer out of her."

Any time of day, I can stop what I'm doing and hear my mother singing. She sang all the time—while she was cooking, while she was cleaning, while she was obediently going about the business of doing whatever my father ordered her to do. It's strange that she lives in Arizona now; "By the Time I Get to Phoenix" was one of her favorite songs.

Before she met my father, Ma had been a nightclub singer. She'd been thin and pretty enough to catch the eye of the men who killed time getting sloshed in nearby gin mills. Ma didn't believe in keeping herself pure, and by the time she was thirteen or fourteen, her mother felt she'd ruined her reputation and disowned her. Around that time, Ma got involved with a guy named Bob King—tall, with blond hair and hazel eyes. Bob King was a criminal, and before Ma turned fourteen he'd landed himself in prison. That's when my father met her.

Music was her escape. It was a refuge, the only home to be relied on by a girl who'd been tossed out at thirteen, and whose husband regularly beat her senseless. She'd sing songs—country-western songs—about places she'd never seen and the true love she'd not yet found. The songs were sad, and when she sang them, they made you feel sad, too.

You could try to talk to her when she was singing, but it was no use. She wouldn't hear you; she was lost in her song. I could tap her on the arm for an hour and a half, trying to get her attention. "Ma, Ma, would you listen to me for a minute? I have something to tell you." But it never worked. She wouldn't answer. She wouldn't even look at me.

Ma can be a little slow. Back then, even in the best of times, she wasn't really on the ball. Unlike my father, Ma is not a controlling person.

Because there were so many of us, she couldn't control us, so she didn't even try. She shut down.

As far back as I can remember, my mother was always scared. I'm sure she felt guilty about us. After all, she stood by and watched while we got beaten to within an inch of our lives. But she was scared of something else, too. She'd get defensive if you brought up something from the past. One of us kids would ask her, "Ma, what was it like when you met Dad? Where were you?" She'd just refuse to answer. Even though she'd clam up, there'd be a catch in her voice, a slight hesitation, like she was aching to get something out, but couldn't. I think she felt a need to reveal things that she knew would create unpleasant consequences. So much pressure must have been building up inside of her. She wanted to relieve herself of all that guilt; she just didn't know how.

Any time she realized she'd done something wrong, she'd put her hand over her mouth and make a face, like a guilty kid caught with her hand in the cookie jar, almost as if she were saying, "Oops!". She tried to avoid confrontation. I think she was afraid of me. Maybe she realized, as I've always believed, that I was a little bit sharper than my brothers and sisters, and she was worried that I might catch on to the game she was playing and confront her. This was her game: She'd pretend to protect us and we, her children, in turn would pretend that she was actually going to. This was not my imagination. She'd even say it: "I'm going to protect you, Wayne, but you'd better behave or else I'm going to tell your father." Of course, she never really protected us. Yet she remained, in the eyes of her children, an innocent victim.

She had us all believing that. She's a great singer. She's a great mother. There's no mother better than your mother—that was her story. This was the same woman who never admitted she'd deserted her kids even when I had proof she'd done that, and on several occasions. And it wasn't a selfless thing she did—leaving us. She'd left us because of her own needs.

My brothers and sisters bought into her story; they considered our mother a perfect angel. After all, hadn't she suffered at the hands of our father just like the rest of us? No one defended her as vehemently as Brian did. "Ma's a saint," he'd say. He never realized that she left him alone when he was three months old. He had no idea that she'd abandoned him. It seemed that my other brothers and sisters felt more or less the same way.

For years I believed her, too. Maybe because I *had* to believe she was a good mother. I didn't have anything else. When I started to realize that she was guilty, too, it completely changed how I felt. I had thought she was deserving of my love because of what she'd had to endure at my father's hands—as if we were all in the same boat, Ma and her brutalized kids against our terrible father. But what if that wasn't true? What if, in her own way, she was his accomplice?

The first time I was rushed to the hospital, I was three-and-a-half years old. My father was cursing and shouting as he drove. "What's wrong with that kid?" he kept screaming. Then he turned and glared at me sitting in the back seat. "Don't get sick on me in the damned car, you hear me?"

I heard him, but I wasn't sure there was very much I could do about it. My stomach was bubbling and churning. I was nauseated and felt like throwing up again, but I held it in because of what would happen to me if I made a mess in the car. Ma wasn't looking at me. She was more worried about my father's driving; he was so riled up, he didn't seem to be paying much attention to the road.

When I wasn't throwing up, I had diarrhea—in my pants, in my bed, everywhere. When I wasn't throwing up or having diarrhea, I was getting nosebleeds. Once the blood started flowing it was impossible to stop it for an hour. It was as if I was leaking out all my insides. Some days I couldn't keep anything in my stomach. Just as soon as I managed to put a bit of moldy toast in my stomach I'd begin to gag and retch. I was thirsty all the time. I could drink a gallon of water and I'd still be thirsty. I kept asking Ma, "What's wrong with me?" But Ma didn't have an answer. Ma never did.

I'd never been in a hospital before. I was more scared of going to the hospital than I was of being sick. Once I went in I was sure they wouldn't let me out. I was going to die in there. My father wanted nothing to do with doctors and hospitals—all he could think about was how much it was going to cost him. You had to be dying before he'd consider taking you to a hospital. So that's what I thought was happening to me: I was dying. I was too little to put up a fight. I couldn't stop them from taking me, but when I glanced back at my house as we pulled out of the driveway, I thought: I'll never see my home again.

Sure, some of my brothers and sisters had been to the hospital and come home. Susan used to tell me how, when she was three, she'd had pneumonia and couldn't breathe, and how no one thought she'd make it. My younger sister Sheila went to the hospital, too, and nearly died from blood poisoning because of a little cut. Then there was the time my father threw hot oil on my brother Christopher and gave him third-degree burns. But just because my brothers and sisters had come out alive, it didn't mean I would.

They laid me on a cot in a room with yellow walls. There was a bright light mounted on the ceiling pointing straight into my eyes. A doctor stood over me, rubbing my belly and asking me, "Does it hurt here?"

My father had put on his "out in public" face of fatherly concern. "I don't understand, he shits all the time. I say 'boo' and he shits."

"He's going to have to stay here a few days while we run some tests," the doctor said.

I started crying. "I want to go home, I don't want to stay here."

"You shut up and listen to the doctor." My father looked like he was glad to get rid of me.

I didn't know when it was day or night, so I don't know how long I was there. I was put in a room with two or three other kids. One of them cried for what seemed like days.

As abruptly as I had gotten there, my parents showed up to take me home. The doctor said I had a "nervous condition." At the age of three, I didn't know what that meant. Neither did my father. He shook his head and muttered. "This is what I'm paying good money for?"

I guess I did have a nervous condition, and I think maybe deep down I knew what was wrong, but I was too young to put it into words. It took me years to figure it out.

Every time my father came near me, I was terrified. I knew he was going to hurt me and I didn't know what to do or where to turn. I was sick from the fear. At three, I was afraid almost all the time.

I remember the feeling of being at home at the end of the day and hearing the crunching of the gravel when my father pulled in the driveway. Even today the sound of tires rolling slowly on gravel is to me the most horrible sound in the world.

Sometimes we'd get lucky and he'd be drunk and come home and go straight to bed. Or else he'd ignore us and fight with my mother, instead. Other times he'd think he was still in the bar, ready to rumble with whoever was ready and willing. He got into a lot of make-believe barroom brawls, and put me or one of my brothers—little kids—in the role of the other guy.

If you tried to defend yourself, that got him madder. "Oh, so you're putting your hands up to me? Is that how it is? Okay, you want to go at it with me?" And then he'd go back to hitting and punching—whatever was available, whatever was defenseless and smaller than him. That was the routine—a beating a day—and I came to expect it.

If he came in late at night and had gotten drunk, he'd sleep late the next morning. That was okay, because usually it meant he'd be in such a hurry to get to work that he couldn't beat anyone. "I ain't got time to pound you now," he'd tell me, "so you're going to have to wait until I get home, and then I'm going to pound you into the ground." I'd think about that all day long, sick with worry and fear, my stomach in knots. I'd try to think about anything else, but it never worked. My mind always came back to the beating I knew was coming.

It went on like this day after day throughout my childhood.

I grew up on the top of a hill at the dead end of a cow path in a northern Massachusetts town called Methuen. From the highway it looked like an abandoned road where a poor farmer might have a little shack and a garden. There were no other roads in sight, there were no other houses, no neighbors. It was like a prison.

The road that led to my house was only wide enough for one car to pass. If you tried backing out, you were sure to end up trapped in one of the four-foot muddy ditches my father had dug on either side of the road for that very purpose.

Our home was situated in a large open space surrounded by woods so thick they were like prison walls. The house sat on cement blocks; a pipe underneath ran from the toilet to the edge of an embankment, where it spilled all the waste into the woods. Whenever you went into the yard, you could smell the stench of all the waste as it kept piling up.

A small, rocky hill stood about fifty feet from the house. In the summer we kids sat there all day long, the way city kids sit on a stoop. But unlike those kids, our hill was our whole world.

There were fun times, mostly when my father wasn't around. It was a pretty big hill. In the summer, we climbed trees. In the winter, we'd hop on a log and go sledding. We'd sled naked sometimes; it felt incredibly free. All year 'round, we'd wrestle—all of us, even the girls. We were pretty wild kids.

We didn't have any toys, but we made up games. We'd pick out rocks that kind of looked like cars, and play something we called "rock cars." We'd drive our little cars around, and that was pretty cool. We'd drive around rocks that looked like trucks, too. Those would make more noise. One time my father kept some horses at the house, and we would dip a stick in the manure. The person with the stick would be "it" and would chase all the other ones around trying to tag them with it.

If my father wasn't home by five-thirty, we'd get to stay in the yard a little longer. Some of the kids were so petrified of him, they'd go inside anyway. Others—me included—stayed outside playing rock cars or chasing each other around, or just looking at the stars.

We couldn't even imagine what the outside world was like. We simply had no conception of it. We wanted to get out, but until each of us started going to school we had zero idea of what "out" was. Our exposure to the outside world was nil. As with Dorothy in the *Wizard of Oz*, for us home was a safety net. It might have been like a prison, but the idea of getting out was unimaginable. Home was where we belonged.

No one got into our place unless my father said so, and no one got out either. He put up gates across the road leading up to our house. The first "gate"—three huge rocks supporting a rusted pipe—was about a quarter of a mile off the main road. He put up wooden posts, too. He probably had ten signs posted at this gate: *No Trespassing. Keep Out. Beware of Dog. No Hunting. No Fishing.* It all added up to one giant "NO."

Once you got past the first gate, you came to another set of boulders. There were posts on both sides of the road there too, with the same signs: *No Trespassing. No Fishing. Keep Out.* He strung a chain across the road and hooked it to the poles. Depending on his mood, he'd fortify the gates with boards and logs, as well. Those gates stayed up for a very long time.

By the time I was three-and-a-half, the gates were in place and the ditches were dug. There was only one way in or out, and it was controlled by my father.

Like a squadron of soldiers on an active front line, we were required to be on the alert at all times. In the mornings, after my father got the car started to drive to work, he'd call out for us to open the gates. The older boys would roll back the boulders to allow him to pass. Even when I was old enough to help them with this task, we could just barely handle those big rocks. So we'd open the gates, leaving the first one open, and then running to open the second one. He wouldn't leave until he'd made sure we'd shut both gates properly. He'd just sit in his car at the end of the road and watch us in the rearview mirror.

When he came home from work, the same sequence happened again, only in reverse. We had to keep track of what time he'd be home. It was always around four or five in the afternoon, but it could vary by an hour or more, so we'd have to listen for the sound of his car approaching. If he pulled up to the first gate and we weren't there, and he had to blow his horn to get our attention, severe beatings were sure to follow.

So we'd all have to run down and open the gates and then shut them after he passed. The gates were always locked. He didn't want anybody coming in. Putting barbed wire around the place would have amounted to the same thing. In some ways, it was like living in a concentration camp, and he was like a Nazi driving in to take command. The gate opened and the gate shut. Things were exactly that way until I was fifteen years old. We were all very scared and very obedient. We'd do anything to avoid the beatings.

I could say I hate that place. But when I drive through it these days, I know that's a lie. I see how beautiful Methuen is, with its lush, old trees, its sparkling rivers, its neat green farms. It's a peaceful, radiant town. But when I think of all the horrifying, hideous things that happened there, the beauty slams shut like the lid of a spring-loaded chest. The beauty becomes the background to a nightmare.

From the time I was a baby to about the age of fourteen, I was hungry all the time. My hunger made me feel queasy and dizzy, and hunger pangs were just a normal part of my life. I thought of food constantly, and when I smelled good food, it drove me crazy.

It wasn't that there wasn't enough to eat. There was always food around. But my father had rules about who could eat what, how much, and when. My father, Ma, and, later, my two older brothers (once they were old enough to work for him) all ate steak. My father would go to the store, buy a nice thick cut, and get it wrapped in that crisp paper that butchers use. (I loved the sound of that paper being opened up.)

Those of us who were too young to work ate mostly hard, moldy bread with peanut butter and jelly, bread that was supposed to be fed to pigs. The bakeries would take unsold bread off the shelf every day and store it on racks in their back rooms, sometimes for months. For three dollars, a farmer could load a pickup truck full of the stuff. My father could buy enough with a quarter to fill up his trunk.

At home, my brothers and sisters and I would stack it in plastic garbage cans. We called it "pig bread," and we had it every day. We ate it with our soup. We cut the mold off and put it in the toaster. On the days we didn't have hamburger soup, we had it with peanut butter, or we'd make ketchup or mayonnaise sandwiches. There was always plenty of that, too.

(Thinking back, I wonder whether that stuff was poisonous. If it was, my family is living proof that you can eat it and live to tell.)

Starving and skinny as we were, we'd watch my parents and the oldest kids with big eyes as they devoured a juicy steak or some chicken wings.

Like starving dogs, we waited for my father to throw us a bone. When he did, the others would fight over it, pushing each other out of the way. Naturally, because they were bigger and more agile, the older kids always got these scraps first. Susan was the quickest. By the time she was finished with a chicken bone, it was *gone*—meat, gristle, bone and all.

I watched, but I couldn't bring myself to dive in with them, even though I was dying for a taste of that meat. The idea of getting down on my hands and knees and fighting for scraps of food made me sick. It just wasn't fair.

Suppertime was torture. I didn't know which was worse, starving half the time or actually getting to sit down and eat. It was okay if I could see my father, but if he was behind me, I knew I was in for it. He'd walk behind me—back and forth—like a drill sergeant. "Hurry up and eat!" he'd shout. "Hurry up so you can get the hell out of this kitchen."

I wolfed down my food so fast I couldn't even taste it. I didn't dare look up because if he caught me I'd be in trouble. It was always so quiet; all you could hear was the sound of everyone chewing. He'd take a few steps forward, a few steps back. Then he was quiet.

Then—bang!—he'd hit me hard on the back of the head as I was trying to swallow. I'd start to cry as I was choking and gagging, and he'd keep hitting me. I was starving and crying and I couldn't eat. Then suppertime was over.

One day I was with my father in the car when he stopped in front of Herb's Fish Market in Haverhill, a town five or six miles down the road from where we lived. I was five years old. He went in to buy some food while I sat waiting in the car. When he came out, he had a piece of fried fish and French fries. The aroma just knocked me over. Smelling it was like I'd died and gone to heaven. Then he got in the car and sat there eating. And I had to sit there and watch him and try not to get dizzy from the aroma. Finally, he remembered that I was there and he let me have some French fries and a bit of the fish skin. If he had said to me, "Hey, Wayne, I'll give you the fish and chips or I'll buy you a brand-new bike—your choice," I'd have taken the fish. That was how much I wanted it. I can still close my eyes and smell those fish and chips.

We had a television set, but we weren't supposed to watch it, even when my father was gone. My mother, though, defied him and watched it anyway. (She was addicted to soap operas.) So sometimes I'd watch soap operas with her, but she always made sure to shut it off in time for it to cool off before he got home.

Even with all his rules and restrictions, I still managed to see a number of shows, like *The Brady Bunch*—an amazing experience for me. For us it could have been a cartoon, because nothing on that show resembled anything in our lives. The Bradys were supposed to be the all-American perfect family—nice, sweet people who weren't fighting with each other all the time. I didn't believe *any* people lived that way. I thought that they were just not real people. It was all a big lie. Families didn't act that way. I couldn't imagine a father coming home from work and walking in the house and saying to his wife, "Hi, sweetheart, how was your day today?" What father sat down and talked to his kids to find out how they were doing? What father took his kids seriously? Things like that didn't happen. That wasn't reality.

Winters were always bad—the most miserable season of all. In winters my father would get laid off and we'd live off unemployment. That meant he was around all the time, and it was torture. We couldn't even cough without getting punched in the head.

Once, when my sister Gail did something wrong, my father cut her hair off—shaved her head right to the skin, and then made her go to school bald. He tried to do the same with Sheila when she got on his nerves. He grabbed her by the hair and began beating her up, kicking her again and again in the stomach with his heel. Then he sat down and squeezed her head between his legs. Once he had her trapped like that, he twisted strands of her hair around his fingers with one hand while holding her head down with the other. He was determined to rip her hair out of her head. And she had such beautiful hair, long and thick and dark. But he grabbed too much of it at a time, so he couldn't rip it out. In frustration he clamped her hair between his teeth and tried to yank it out that way. She still has a bald place—a scar on her scalp about an inch long (and about a tooth-and-a-half wide). She called what he did "derooting." My father "derooted" her. No one, I noticed, ever got derooted on *The Brady Bunch*.

I also never saw an episode of *The Brady Bunch* where discipline was enforced with a spatula. But a metal spatula was a regular feature of The Theodore Show. That was my father's inspiration when he wanted to beat us up in a different way. He liked to use the spatula when he was tired and wanted to get all the beatings out of the way in one fell swoop. He would make us all line up and each of us would have to put out our hands and keep them out. And then he'd choose one of us to mete out the punishment. "John," he'd say, "give them thirty whacks on each hand." But if John didn't whack us hard enough, my father would rip the spatula away from him and whack *him* over the head. He could tell whether the blows were hard enough by the sound of the crack against the skin. "*This* is how I want it done," he'd say, and then he'd show us.

If you were on the receiving end, the last thing you'd want to do is pull your hand away at the last moment. If you did that, he'd beat you over the head with the spatula. If he missed your hand, the same thing would happen—a whack over the head. If you did something wrong, you'd get fifty smacks on each hand automatically. My hands often were black, blue, and blistered. One day he broke a spatula on me. He was so angry about having to go out and buy another spatula that he gave me a beating with his hands. Our bodies were covered with welts and bruises pretty much all the time. Sometimes the pain was fierce and I couldn't concentrate on anything else, but there were a lot of days when the pain was more bearable, so that I began to think of it as normal—like there was always going to be some pain, one or another part of me was always going to be aching or throbbing, but that was just how it was. I'd just be grateful that every so often I could take my mind off the hurt and think about something else.

I didn't know much about God or religion, but I knew people celebrated Christmas and went to church to pray to God. God was supposed to be all-powerful. That was what I'd heard on the radio and TV. But where was God? And if he was so powerful why didn't He help us? I used to pray to the stars because I thought that God was on one of them. I always wanted to know exactly which star God was on. I'd ask God for things like clothes, but mainly I prayed not to get beaten up. I never really, truly believed that I'd ever get anything I asked for, though. God wasn't going to listen to me because of all of the things I'd done wrong. I was a bad kid. It wasn't my father's fault; it was *my* fault. I was just a bad kid. He had to do what he had to do.

And that was the only reality I knew.

Until I was ten or eleven, I couldn't stop wetting my bed. I don't know if it was physical or emotional, but I do know that I was very ashamed of it. And every day I got beaten for it. My father would punch my face in, push my head into the wet mattress, and kick the hell out of me. Five in the morning, the old alarm clock by his bed would wake him up. The first thing he'd do when he got out of bed was to check to see if I'd wet the bed. I usually did, but I knew how to hide it if I heard him coming in time. I'd flip the mattress and hide my underwear.

There was a bureau in my bedroom propped up against the bunk bed where I slept. Between the bureau and the wall there was hardly any space. Sometimes, when I slept, I'd put my feet on the bureau. One night when I was seven years old, I accidentally pushed it over with my feet.

When it happened, I thought I was dreaming that my father was coming into the room, but I could barely hear his footsteps; he was very quiet, like he was sneaking up on me. Then I realized it wasn't a dream, and, although I didn't dare open my eyes, I knew he was getting closer. My heart was pounding. Why hadn't I heard the alarm go off? Had I slept through it? Maybe Ma forgot to wind it; then she'd get a pounding, too. The next thing I knew his hand was on my pants. I knew what he was looking for. "You dirty son of a bitch! You pissed the bed!"

He grabbed me by the hair and yanked hard. Then he hurled me out of the top bunk bed and slammed me down on the floor. I was praying he wouldn't hurt me too badly.

He started with a couple of kicks to the stomach, and then another one to the head while I was still on my back. Then he dragged me around the floor. "You pissed in the bed, you son of a bitch! You pissed in the bed!"

The bedroom was very small. This made it hard for him to beat me up, because he didn't have the space to throw a hard punch or get in a good kick. So he picked me up by the hair, threw me back on the bunk bed and smashed my face in the wet mattress to teach me the lesson I never seemed to learn. Then he started pounding me in the back of the head with the side of his fist—never with the knuckles. I think he felt I was doing it on purpose just to make him mad. He didn't realize or didn't care that I couldn't help it. And he hated me, too—more than my brothers and sisters—and just liked to hurt me.

I had no idea why my father hated me so much. If I could make him see that I was trying hard to be a good kid, maybe he would stop doing this to me. No one—not my mother or my brothers or sisters—would come to my rescue.

He went on hitting me on the side and back of my head. By this time the whole house was awake. I knew enough to lie there and take it. If I stood up it would only make him madder. That was showing a sign of strength. That was defying him. I always cried because, unless I cried, he just beat me harder and harder. He needed to know that he'd broken me.

I kept wishing that Ma would help us.

He was hollering for my mother. "Ruth, get in here and clean this piss up!"

She came running and started cleaning with Pine-Sol. But that didn't mean he was through with me. While my mother was busy cleaning, he dragged me out of the bedroom and hauled me into the kitchen, where he started beating me all over again.

My father was hurting his fist, but he wasn't hurting me, because he was hitting iron. I tightened my skin all over and shut my eyes, hard. Then I concentrated as hard as I could until I was able to detach myself. I was floating. I'd escaped back to my safe place, where I could stop time and where my father's punches just passed right through me. He pulled on my hair so hard that I thought he'd yank it right out of my scalp, but I didn't feel that, either. I couldn't feel anything at all. I was just watching him and making sure that that little boy would be okay. He had no power over me as long as I was hidden in my safe place. I just hunkered down and waited until he was through.

Then he flung me back face down on the bed and told me to stay put—"And don't let me catch you moving from there!"

I was really bleeding, especially from my nose. Puffy eyes, scratches on my chin. My hair was a mess.

But I continued to wet the bed for years. I just couldn't help myself, even though I knew I'd face a beating in the morning. To my father's great frustration, beatings didn't do the trick. Nearly every morning I'd wake up, feel the moist sheets, and think, *Oh no, I did it again!* So my father decided to make new rules to stop me from wetting the bed. He told me that I couldn't drink anything after I came home from school. *Nothing.* If I had a peanut butter sandwich for supper, that was it. No water, nothing. The only time I was allowed to drink was in the morning and during the day. On weekends, once the clock had struck twelve in the afternoon, I got no more water. Shut off.

The next night I lay in bed, praying I'd be able to hold it in until morning. But I didn't know how I'd do it. I'd tried to be a good boy before, but then I'd wake up and realize that I'd wet myself and go into a panic. Why couldn't I be a good boy? What was the matter with me?

So much happened to our family that none of us remembered. We didn't want to remember, and that included Brian. He understood that he was messed up, and he suspected it had to do with how we were raised, but finding out the truth was another matter. Even though he had a thousand questions about himself, I don't think he was necessarily ready for the truth. My other brothers and sisters weren't prepared for it, either.

As it turned out, neither was I, but I didn't know this at the time.

Right after I got off the phone with Brian that day I called my mother. This wasn't the first time I'd tried to get my mother to open up. Whenever I'd asked her a question about the past, about what really went on, I'd get a little close to the bone, and she'd run and hide.

"Oh, you're trying to abuse me," she'd say. "You're trying to abuse me." Then she'd hang up on me. I'd have to call her back and reassure her, convince her that I didn't mean any harm, build up her confidence. I could sense that she wanted to tell me certain things—it was in her voice and in her hesitations—but I also knew that she was scared to breathe a word because she realized that she was at least partly responsible for what had happened to us.

I could understand why she'd feel guilty.

But I wouldn't let her off the hook. I kept coming back. I'd tell her, "You know, you keep saying it was the old man's fault, he was the one who was responsible for everything that happened to us." Then I'd ask, "Hey, Ma, what were you doing while all this was going on?" And usually that was when she'd hang up on me.

This time, though, I was determined to get my answers. I knew she might cut me off, but I pressed ahead. After a while she began to talk. And talk. It was probably a relief for her to get it off her chest. Half the time I didn't even know what she was talking about; I was just taking it all in. I didn't want to interrupt, because I didn't want to scare her off. It was as if she was putting together a puzzle in words, so I had to pay careful attention to every little bit and piece of what she was saying.

Then all of a sudden she just blurted out, "He made me plead guilty." Then she caught herself. She must have realized she'd gone too far.

Plead guilty? She didn't say "charges." She didn't say "neglect." She didn't say "for driving a car without a license." She just said, "He made me plead guilty," and then she stopped dead and cut me off and that was it. I couldn't get any more out of her.

I called Brian back. I told him about the strange conversation I'd just had.

Even as I was talking to him I was still sorting out in my mind exactly what my mother had said. I hadn't quite digested it. Brian didn't seem to know what to make of it, either.

It took me about a day to piece it together and then all of a sudden it was as if someone had hit the light switch. *Plead guilty?* Wait a minute, I thought. Plead guilty. The words kept bouncing around in my mind. And I said to myself, if you're going to plead guilty, there must be a charge.

Then I took it a step further. If charges are brought against someone, I thought, it has to be a matter of public record. Even though my mother had clammed up it didn't mean I couldn't find out the truth. There had to be any number of places I could look for this sort of information— newspapers, arrest records, court documents. Why were my parents charged? I needed to know. That was where it started. That's when the door opened.

The woods around our yard were forbidden territory. My father wanted us to live in fear of them, so we'd never want to go into them. He warned us about wild bears that would tear us limb from limb. He told us to be extra careful, because a ferocious mountain lion was running loose in the woods.

My father put such fear in me and my brothers and sisters that the very idea of leaving the yard was scary. But it wasn't the mountain lion we were afraid of. It was him.

Because he was never around during the day, he wasn't actually able to see what we were doing, but we were sure he'd find out everything we did eventually, and we'd get a beating we'd remember for the rest of our lives if we disobeyed. Just to make sure I understood, he beat me up even before I took a single step out of the yard. It was as if he knew better than I did what I was going to do. Even so, I secretly declared war on my father: I was going into the woods—the forbidden territory—anyway.

The first time I took the big step and went into the woods, I was six years old. I felt like I was standing on the edge of a big cliff, staring down into the dark, not able to see the bottom. There wasn't a fence or wall or anything, just a line of trees that marked where the woods began. Beyond the trees, I had no idea what was waiting for me. I couldn't be absolutely sure there was no mountain lion or black bear.

But not knowing what I was going to find only made the woods more appealing. I started off gradually and went in only a little way, so I could get used to the feeling of being where I wasn't supposed to be. It was as if I had one leg over the wall of a prison. I waited until I saw that I was totally alone. I had to be careful no one saw me leave the yard, because my brothers and sisters would rat on me.

But they were sitting on the hill, where they couldn't see me. My father was at work. *Now's the time,* I thought. *I have to do it.* I was scared, but as soon as I was entirely over that imaginary wall, I knew I'd be okay. No mountain lions were going to get me.

I realized I could go a little way and nobody would see me from the yard. I could feel the power, smell the clean scent of freedom, before I was even in the woods.

At first I kind of played around, testing the limits, seeing how far in I dared to go. This went on for a long, long time. One day I'd go four or five trees in, and I'd keep careful track. Then maybe the next day I'd skip the woods. The day after that, I'd go six trees or eight trees deep, until, finally, I was *all the way in.*

Wow, look at all the blueberries! I could hardly believe it! They tasted so good and I could eat as many as I wanted. I could come here almost any day and I'd have food. That was an amazing discovery. My fingers turned blue. The woods were full of other food ripe for the taking— tomatoes, peppers, pears, green berries, red raspberries, black raspberries, even fruit that I didn't recognize. It was amazing. Grapevines were growing all over the place. A farmer must have planted them a long time ago. I could feast on as many plump and juicy grapes as my stomach would hold. I'd eat them even before they were ripe. That would take up at least half a day, just eating grapes off the vine. As long as I could come to the woods, I would never be hungry.

The problem was I didn't know what would happen when winter came. I didn't mind being out in the rain, but the freezing cold was something else. I dreaded winters because my father would get laid off from whatever job he happened to be doing at the time—running a bull-dozer, working in a shoe factory, whatever. It basically meant he'd be around more often, and it was too bitterly cold to escape to the one refuge I had.

The north side of the woods was where the blueberry bushes grew. That was the area I favored in summer. Then, in fall, when the fruit was ripening, I headed to the south side of the woods to help myself to the pears. I stayed away from the western part of the woods, though, because there were houses there, and I was afraid somebody would see me. If I was recognized as one of the Theodore kids, I'd be in a lot of trouble. If I ever heard somebody coming, I'd hide. They'd never find me. I could hide just like a deer.

I used to talk to the trees. I imagined they were my friends. I asked them how school was. I asked them what they had to eat that day. Sometimes I punished them for not closing the gate after I got home. I really got the most out of those woods.

But when the light hit the trees at a certain angle, I knew it was time to go. I felt sad, but I knew I'd come back the next day, or the day after that.

The woods never hurt me or made me go hungry or called me names. The woods were like another sort of safe place for me, a sanctuary where my father could never harm me.

In the woods I could be anybody I wanted to be. Sometimes I'd pretend to be an Indian or Tarzan. I'd start to run through the woods so fast a rabbit couldn't keep up. I'd leap over dead trees and run through thick "pricker" bushes—bushes that had sharp branches like the thorns on a rosebush. I got so good I could run right over them in bare feet without a scratch.

It felt so good to lie down on the ground and look up at the sky through the trees. I knew how to let that peacefulness pass into me, like an airplane passes into a cloud.

I was scared in the beginning, but the feeling of freedom was so strong that the fear became secondary. It was like nothing else in the world. Even after I left the woods, I carried that peaceful place with me. I carried the sky that I glimpsed through the treetops with me wherever I went.

I could survive in the woods alone. I didn't know it then, but the woods were teaching me an important lesson: They were testing me, giving me the chance to see if I could make it on my own, if I was willing to risk my father's fury to claim my freedom.

The only thing I was afraid of in the woods was dozing off. I was afraid to take a nap because I didn't want to sleep too long and not make it back before my father got home. Then one day it happened: When I woke up, I couldn't see the sun anymore, and the light coming through the trees told me that it was about five o'clock in the afternoon.

I ran. I tripped over a root and got up again and ran some more. I was out of breath, my chest hurt, but I wasn't going to stop. All I kept thinking about was what would happen if my father caught me. As I got closer to our house I could start to hear the voices of my brothers and sisters sitting up on the hill. Hearing them scared me.

I sneaked up to the edge of the hill, where they couldn't see me but I could see them. For a moment I felt like a prisoner who'd gotten free and was watching the other prisoners who were still behind bars. It made me mad that I had to go back inside and become a prisoner again.

When my father came home from work that night, just as soon as he got out of the car, he went up to each of us and asked, "Who left the yard today?" He only had to take one look at me. His eyes said: I can read you. He knew I was leaving the yard, so he would play a game. He would pick one of my brothers and grab him by the hair and demand to know which one of us had left the yard that day. Right off the bat the victim would blurt out, "Oh, he did it, he did it," pointing at me. So I had to keep my going into the woods a secret. It was survival.

Sometimes my father would take a different tack. He'd pretend to be nice to one of us. He'd say to John or Michael, "Hey, you're a good kid. You're one of my best." He'd hint that if the kid came clean he'd get out of a beating that day. He'd say, "You tell me the truth, and I'll let you off." Usually that would be all it would take. Then it was confession time: The kid would melt. "Dad, guess what?" A lot of times they supplied him with information without being asked, just to please him.

But it was stupid to try. There was really nothing you could do to please him except to rat. You couldn't come home and say, "Look, Dad, I got an A on my report card!" Or, "Look, I raked the whole yard." That never cut it with him. Only ratting did. I hated the whole idea of ratting, what it did to the people who ratted, and what it represented. I was beaten up plenty of times because someone had ratted me out, so I knew what it felt like.

I wouldn't hurt somebody else to do my father a favor. But I understood why his game was so effective. Getting my father to say that you were one of his favorites was better than anything. For that moment, you were singled out as special, and that was an amazing gift. Just the words, "You're my favorite, you're a good boy," were all we wanted. We needed more than anything else his love and approval, and this was the only way we could get it. We all believed that he was a strict father, but not a mean one, not evil.

When one of us told on one of our brothers or sisters, not only did that person not get beaten up, but he or she even got to sit in a special chair and watch everybody else's beatings. My brothers and sisters were so desperate not to get beaten themselves—and probably also to have, just for a moment, a feeling of being treated specially, or maybe even being loved—that they didn't mind watching him beat one of the other kids. But the kid who ratted would get beaten up eventually, too—if not that day, then the next.

It was very important for my father to know everything. He always expected that sooner or later everything would be revealed to him. And there was this sense that if you didn't reveal what you knew he'd find out anyway, and you'd get punished.

So no trust built up among us. There was no one in my family who I could actually count on to be honest with me.

For a long time, I didn't understand why the other kids would tell on me. It wasn't something I would have done. For a while I tried to teach the others not to do it, either. If we stuck together, I'd say, we'd all save ourselves a lot of pain and misery. But it never worked. The fear and the need for attention and approval always won them over.

My father was the center of everything. He was the most powerful man in our universe and we all—even me—had a tremendous need to win his love. No matter what he did, we clung to the idea that there must be some way to get him to show that love to us. It was just that none of us knew how.

"He made me plead guilty."

After that strange conversation with my mother, I was anxious to begin my search. I wanted to know what had happened to all of us when we were kids, and I was determined to get to the bottom of it. At the time, I was living in a town called Atkinson, in southern Massachusetts. It wasn't far from where we'd all grown up and where most of my family still lived, so I didn't think I'd have to go far to find public records about my family. I figured the best place to start was the public library in Lawrence, about a half-hour drive away.

I arrived an hour before it opened at nine. I sat in my truck, sipping lukewarm coffee, waiting for the doors to open. I felt like a private investigator in a movie skulking around after a suspect. At the same time, I had the creepy sensation I was being watched, that there was something dangerous about what I was about to do. The adrenaline was pumping. I was so jumpy I couldn't sit still. The clock on the dashboard seemed frozen at quarter to nine. I stared at the door, willing it to open. But when it finally did, I hung back. I realized that once I'd started this, there was no turning back.

I walked slowly up the stairs to the entrance, feeling nervous and scared, as if I was about to uncover something very big. I couldn't tell exactly what, but it was almost as if I already knew.

I went up to the desk and asked the librarian if I could see all the local newspapers for the years 1958, when I was born, through 1962. I was guessing that the case would have occurred somewhere around then, when I was too young to really know what was going on.

I spent the whole day staring at the computer terminal, scrolling through copies of every newspaper published over those three years, until my eyes were so bleary I could scarcely read the print anymore. And the whole time the words kept echoing in my brain: *He made me plead guilty. He made me plead guilty.* I was determined. I knew it had to be there somewhere. We're talking about a small town. It wasn't like Boston or New York, where people get arrested all the time. Any arrest in Methuen would make the news. So it had to be in the archives somewhere.

By the end of the day I was totally beat. I'd found no mention of any case. The library was getting ready to close, and they asked me to leave. I decided I'd just have to come back the next day for another go at it. And if I didn't find anything the next day, I'd come back the day after that. Sooner or later, I'd find what I was looking for.

My parents didn't have much education. They never talked about school to us. It just wasn't important to them. So what a surprise it was for me when they announced that they were sending me to school when I was six years old. I was excited, but I was also scared. I had no idea what to expect.

I was enrolled in the Pleasant Valley School. To get there, I walked down the road from my house and then a few blocks along a street that ran through Methuen. It was only about a thousand yards from the end of my road to the school, but that first day it could have been a hundred miles. Just being able to walk the length of that road to get to school was strange for me. I didn't know what to expect, and I was too nervous to enjoy the chance to get away from home. From that day on, and for years afterward, that stretch was all I knew of the outside world.

Other kids who lived nearby would be walking in the same direction. I recognized some of them. When I was roaming through the woods I'd sometimes run into a couple of these kids. They came from a big family that lived in a tenement building on the other side of our property. You couldn't see their place because of all the trees in the way, though. Their father was a carpenter. I don't know how many kids there were altogether, but even as a kid I could tell they were probably as poor as we were. But there was a big difference between them and us. Their clothes, like ours, were a little shabby, but you could tell that their parents had gone to some trouble to dress them. They probably didn't have much more money than we did, but the kids seemed to be pretty happy. I wondered whether their dad beat them like our dad did.

But what really amazed me were the kids I'd never seen before. How much better dressed they were. Some of them wore clothes that matched, like the socks were the same color as their shirts. Some of the girls wore earrings and bracelets. What's more, these kids were clean and their hair wasn't messy or grimy, like ours. We never combed our hair—we never needed to; my father used to give us the shortest crew cuts with an instrument that looked like horse shears. Even if I could have let my hair grow, I had nothing to comb it with. I'd have had to make do with a horse brush. That was because my father made sure that there was a brush for the horse but not for us. My father kept his own comb in his back pocket. (He didn't always use it for his hair, though. Sometimes, when he was beating us, he'd reach for it and break it over our heads. He went through a lot of combs that way.)

When I compared these other kids to myself—with my ragged, dirty clothes, clutching my brown paper bag with a ketchup sandwich in it— they seemed pretty high-class. We were just the poor, filthy kids who lived on the hill in the woods. We had to conclude the others were all millionaires.

n the summer we were naked half the time. Our clothes lay in the bathroom in a heap about four feet wide and four feet deep, reeking of the accumulated dirt, soil, food, and waste that resulted from a lot of kids in various stages of potty training and rough play. Sometimes I'd see maggots crawling in the pile.

Before the school term started my father would gather up the pile, split it into a dozen green plastic trash bags, and drive my mother to the Laundromat. He'd enlist one of my brothers or sisters—usually someone older than me, like Susan or Joseph—to accompany her. They weren't there to help her, though. They were there to watch her to make sure she didn't run away.

I was never really part of this laundry trip, but I could only imagine the looks on the faces of the other customers at the Laundromat, as my mother pulled out one stained and dirt-and-feces encrusted pair of pants after another. There were so many clothes to wash, she'd take over a whole row of washing machines. Even then, she'd end up overloading them so that the clothes never came out clean enough. They still stank when she brought them home, they just didn't stink quite as much.

Not so with my father's clothes, though. My mother washed his clothes in the sink every day. She made sure that his shirts and trousers were crisp and clean, and nicely ironed. They were never allowed to pile up, like ours did.

Early in the morning on the first day of school, we'd all gather around my mother, waiting for her to divvy up the clothes. "John, here's a shirt for you. Joseph, here's a pair of pants for you. Those don't fit? Well, you'll have to make do. . . ." Once we'd gotten our clothes for school we'd have to make them last until the next washing day—which could be a week, or, if my father didn't want to bother, two weeks away. Then we were forced to rely on the clothes pile again and change one set of dirty clothes for another.

I'd usually get just a regular flannel button-up shirt and pants cut high above the ankles. The pants were "floods," hemmed so high you could wade around in a flood without getting them wet. The kids at school made fun of me. "Hey, Theodore," they'd shout. "What are you waiting for, a flood?"

I felt so humiliated.

When the weather got colder my mother gave me sweaters with holes in the elbows and sleeves too short to pull down to keep my hands warm. When it got really cold, we wore GoodWill- or Salvation Army-type coats. I remember going to school in a girl's old wool coat with black buttons and a fake fur collar.

The shoe situation wasn't any better. I wore worn-out vinyl shoes with no socks, or with one short sock and one long one, or socks that didn't quite come up over the heel. And they hardly ever matched. In winters my feet would be freezing even after I got inside the classroom. Shoes were a special obsession for my father. No one could wear shoes inside the house. We'd have to line all the shoes up on the porch, and if the shoes weren't lined up perfectly, my father would go into a rage.

My father bought us cheap hats that were too big for us. When he gave us a hat he'd say, "If you take this off before you get to school, I'll know it." I believed him—I believed everything he told us—but I used to take the hat off, anyway, and the girl's coat, too, and hide them in the woods. Then I'd pick them up on the way home. One day I got ratted on by one of my brothers and my father beat me for it. I realized then that he *did* know everything that was going on; he had his spies! So after that I had to wear the hat and the coat. The hat, especially, was mandatory. That made things worse for us at school. My father knew we hated them. He knew the kids would laugh at us.

I saw the new parka jackets hanging in the cloakroom. I watched the "rich" kids stuff warm mittens into their jacket pockets. As soon as there was snow on the ground, I'd see boots all lined up on the shelf in the classroom closet under the coat hooks. All those nice boots fascinated me. Seeing how well-dressed these kids were, I thought, *Why them? Why do I have to wear old, smelly clothes and worn-out shoes?* When I was by myself, I pretended it didn't matter, but when I saw the other kids, I compared myself to them and felt embarrassed all over again. I didn't know who to be mad at—them or my parents. Mostly, I think, I was mad at myself, because I felt so unable to change my situation.

The Pleasant Valley School was a drab, gray two-story building. I was all right the first day I walked to school, because I had my brothers and sister with me. All of a sudden, though, while standing in the schoolyard waiting to go in for the first time, I was terrified. I had no idea what to expect. To me it seemed that all the other first-graders knew each other. I felt completely left out. I wanted to be back home, sitting on our hill or running in the woods. At least I knew the woods. I could survive in the woods.

My older sister Susan told me I had to be at the door as soon as school let out and then we were all to go straight home. On my first day, I had no chance to ask any questions because she and my brothers immediately disappeared in the crowd and left me alone. I followed a teacher and a bunch of the youngest kids inside and down a long hallway with shiny hardwood floors.

We went up a stairway to the classroom. I had no idea what else was in the school. I had no concept of where the other classrooms were, where my brothers and my sister had gone. But although I was still a little scared, I was excited, too, at seeing so many kids and being in this huge school building. It was a new world for me.

The classroom was a large, very bright room with big windows covered with wire mesh. The ceilings were very high. I'd never seen anything like it before in my life. It was the opposite of I was used to. My house had low ceilings, dark rooms, and small windows that were always covered. And, unlike these shiny hardwood floors, our floors were made of plywood.

The wooden desks were square with metal legs. Metal strips linked each desk to the one in front of it and the one in back. The teacher, Mrs. Cole, told me to sit in a desk in the second row from the front, second seat from the left. She didn't say it, but she'd put me there so she could keep an eye on me. She'd decided I was bad just by looking at me.

Four rows of kids sat behind me. They could see me, and (unless I turned around, which wasn't easy) I couldn't see them. This bothered me a lot. I didn't want anybody behind me. I could hear them whispering, and while I couldn't hear what they were saying I was sure they were talking about me. And I had the feeling that what they had to say wasn't very good. The one good thing about my seat was that I could see out the window and watch what was going on in the playground. But each time I let my eyes stray the teacher would catch me and warn me to look straight ahead.

Mrs. Cole took her place in front behind a huge wooden desk. Her hair was piled on top of her head. I kept staring at it. I wasn't used to seeing women with hairdos.

Behind her was a blackboard with big letters and words on it. I'd seen signs on our property and signs along the street and letters on the economy-size packages of food we had at home, but I didn't know what letters actually *were*. We didn't have pencils or paper at home. No one ever wrote anything in our house. Maybe my father did once in a while for business but I never saw him do it. Certainly no one ever read anything.

Mrs. Cole began to go from desk to desk, distributing No. 2 pencils and erasers and pads of lined paper. I thought that was pretty cool. Nobody had ever given me anything before. My parents never gave us any toys, so a pencil and paper was a big deal, even if I wasn't sure what I was going to do with them. When the teacher went back to the blackboard and started pointing to the letters and saying their names and telling us to repeat them, though, I didn't have a clue what this was about or what she wanted me to do. I had no idea what reading was, and I barely had any idea what writing was. It never occurred to me that I might write, myself.

I discovered that the bathroom was in the basement, two flights down those creaky wooden stairs. When I had to go, I did it almost in secret. I'd tiptoe so I wouldn't make any noise. I didn't want to be noticed. I'd try to go down there when there were no other kids around. I thought if I was quiet and no one noticed me, nothing bad would happen.

I'd never been in a bathroom with functioning plumbing and a toilet that actually flushed. It looked to me like something from a science-fiction movie. It was probably just an ordinary bathroom, but the size of it, the pipes on the ceiling, the shiny white urinals, the green-and-white tiled walls—all of these were from outer space. From the urinals to the stalls with doors to the row of white porcelain sinks—everything was so bright, clean, and spotless. The best thing about the bathroom was the smell of the disinfectant when the urinal flushed. At home, even if the toilet was working (and it usually wasn't), there was only enough water to flush it every two or three days.

In those first few weeks I had a little trouble understanding what Mrs. Cole was trying to tell us. I didn't have any idea what she wanted me to do. I knew I was there to learn something, but I didn't know how to go about it. She'd go to the blackboard and begin to write on it. "Pay attention, class," she'd say. "I want you to do what I'm doing." Soon the blackboard would be filled with letters of the alphabet. I looked to my left and then to my right and was amazed to see my classmates diligently copying the letters on their sheets of lined paper. No matter what kind of lines I put down nothing came out remotely like the letters Mrs. Cole was writing on the blackboard. After a few minutes I'd fallen so hopelessly behind that I gave up and just started doodling.

Then Mrs. Cole turned around and said something that filled me with dread. "Okay, class, now I want to take a look at what you've done."

She began with the front row. Each kid would nervously show her his paper and she'd make a comment and go on to the next one. I kept my head down. My heart was pounding. *She's going to think I'm stupid when she sees my paper.* How could I tell her I'd never used a pencil before in my life? The other kids would laugh at me.

Finally she came to me. She took my hand away from the paper and held it up. "You seem to be having some trouble here, Wayne," she said, but not unkindly.

She stepped behind me and asked me to pick up my pencil. When I did, she placed her hand on mine and began to guide my hand—and the pencil—to help me form the capital letter "A." But I could hardly concentrate on what my hand was doing when I was so busy taking in the smell of her perfume. She smelled so good. It wasn't a smell I was used to. And she was so close, too, almost as if she was about to take me in her arms.

"That's good, Wayne," she said, jolting me out of my daydream. "Now I want you to make another column over there—that's right—and we're going to do the same thing, only this time I want you to write a small 'a.'" And again, with her hand guiding mine, I somehow managed to form a small "a." Once she was convinced I could master this lesson, she moved on to "B." And that was how she taught me to write.

I liked learning how to write for a lot of reasons. For one thing, I was proud of my new skill. For another, I was getting special attention—and some affection—that I never got at home.

All the same, Mrs. Cole could be mean. No matter how hard she worked to teach me how to read and write, she made it clear that she didn't really like me. She didn't like any of the Theodore kids. Nobody at school did. Nobody liked us because of how we smelled and how we dressed. We were different from the other kids.

Even after failing to find any reference to my family's case in the library archives, I wasn't discouraged. I just knew it was just going to take more work than I'd expected. So the next day I went back to the library. This time I asked to see the microfilms of papers from 1961 through 1968. I was ready to spend as many hours or days as it took, but, just as I started in, I had an inspiration. Why not go over to the courthouse in Lawrence and find out if I could get information there? It would be a lot easier than plowing through eight years of newspapers.

By the time I reached the courthouse, though, I wasn't very hopeful. It struck me that maybe, in spite of what my mother had said, there was no such record.

I stepped inside the courthouse and my heart sank. There were so many offices. Dozens of people milled around looking like they'd been waiting forever for someone to see them. I couldn't find a friendly face anywhere. *Still,* I thought, *now that I'm here I might as well give it a shot.*

I found a door labeled Clerk's Office and walked in. I sat down and watched the clerks for a while, trying to figure out which one looked the most sympathetic and helpful. I settled on a middle-aged woman with a pleasant smile and a soft voice. Her fingers were smudged with ink and she wore a gold locket engraved with the letter "G." I had the feeling that if I was friendly and could make her understand my situation a little, she might be willing to help me out. When she asked what I wanted, I had my story ready. I'd rehearsed it all the way over to the courthouse.

"My family is in pain," I said—I could see I had her undivided attention—"and we want to learn the truth about something that happened with our parents a long time ago, sometime between 1958 and 1962."

"What about them?"

"They were arrested."

"For what?"

"That's what I've come here to find out." I explained that we had no hope of getting the truth out of our parents.

I could see the compassion in her eyes. She hesitated for a moment and then told me to wait, gesturing to the dusty volumes lining the shelves behind her. I could only assume they contained court records for the years in question. Now my heart was pumping harder than ever. I'd gone into the courthouse feeling hopeless, but seeing those records gave me a boost more powerful than any amount of caffeine or alcohol could have.

She knew exactly where to look. She got up on a small stool and took a book off the shelf. I could make out the dates "1960–1961" on the binding. As she slowly turned pages, licking her fingers each time she did so, she held the book so that I could see it if I wanted, but she was careful not to make it obvious to prevent everyone else in the room from catching on to what she was doing.

January, February, March, June, July. She flipped through the pages, scanning the index of cases—nothing. I kept rubbing my palms against my trousers because they were so sweaty. I felt like I had a winning lottery ticket but had to wait to have the numbers confirmed. My heart fell when I saw her shrugging. Was she going to give up? No, I thought, I couldn't allow that. She had to keep going. "Could you please, please just look a little further? See whether you can find anything in August."

She turned the page. And there it was. Suddenly I felt so weak I could barely stand. My hands were shaking. "Yes, here it is," she said, sounding a little surprised herself. She read off a docket number and a date—Tuesday, August 29, 1961. She wrote the information on a piece of paper and handed it to me. She said she was sorry, that was as much as she could do. But I was elated. She'd given me all I needed.

The first time I snuck into my parents' bedroom when they weren't there I noticed a pair of my father's trousers on the floor. I put my hand in the pants pockets and grasped hold of some change. I took a handful of coins. It wasn't something I'd been planning. It was just an impulse. I'd only taken a couple of dimes and nickels and some pennies—enough to buy a few hot balls at the candy store on my way home from school.

Now when I think back, I know that wasn't why I did it. A lot of times when people steal it's because they want to snatch back some power in their lives. This was true for me. I needed to claim some of the power my father had stolen from me. I didn't think of it as stealing. I was just trying to make things more equal, make myself feel that I was worth something, that I had at least a little bit of control over my own actions.

He wasn't going to miss a few coins, but after I took them, I wanted to take more. My father always carried a wad of cash—hundreds of dollars for the week's earnings—in his pants pocket. *Do I have the guts?* I wondered.

One night I stayed up late, waiting for everybody else to go to bed. I could hear my parents in the next room. Only a plywood partition separated my bedroom from theirs. Usually my mother was the first to fall asleep. As soon as she began to snore, though, my father would whack her. "Cut it out, Ruth," he'd say, "you're snoring!" If, when she started snoring again, he didn't whack her, that told me that he was out, too. I could hear him snoring and grinding his teeth. That was my signal: I climbed out of bed and crawled out of the room, quiet as a cat. Then

I peeked around the corner so I could look straight into my parents' bedroom. If I saw my father's face, I turned right around. I couldn't have done it with him facing me, even if his eyes were closed. All he had to do was open his eyes and catch me there and I would have been a goner. But his face was turned away from me, so I proceeded.

He always rolled his pants up before going to sleep and stuck them under the bed, so I knew exactly where to go. I crawled slowly toward the bed. As soon as I was under it and had dug my hand into his pants pocket, I heard him say something.

I nearly jumped out of my skin. I was petrified. I couldn't move. I didn't even want to breathe. For a moment I thought he knew I was there, but as I listened I realized he must be talking to my mother. She was answering in grunts and groans.

How long was he going to keep talking? My leg was cramping up, but if I tried to move it I might make a noise, so I tried to block out the discomfort. My hand was still in his pants pocket. I didn't even want to think about what would happen if he discovered me. I waited and waited, and he kept talking. But now my mother wasn't making a sound. She was fast asleep. After a while he began snoring, too. And then, with my heart pounding, I decided if I was going to do this thing I'd better do it now, before he woke up again.

I knew he kept his wallet in a different pocket from the one in which he kept the change. Very slowly, sucking my breath in, I pulled a bill out. One was enough. I wasn't going to press my luck any further.

When I got back to my room I tried to read the number on the bill but I couldn't see it; it was too dark. I could just make out the number "5." Five was safe. I didn't think he'd miss it. Except for my jaunts into the woods, this was the boldest thing I'd ever done against him. I'd proved to myself that I could challenge him on his own turf. I'd pulled this off right under his bed while he was asleep. I'd proved that he wasn't all-powerful, as he wanted us to think.

So I was pretty pleased with myself—at least until I woke up the next morning and found out what I had.

I reached under the bureau and pulled out my loot: I couldn't believe it. It wasn't a five; it was a fifty! *A fifty!* I couldn't believe it. I was scared and nervous, but at the same time I was deliriously happy. I quickly hid it under the bureau, knowing I'd have to think of a better hiding place the next day.

Then I heard the door fly open and my father walked in. He hadn't been gone more than an hour. He must have discovered the fifty was gone on his way to work. And he knew who took it. He came right after me and beat me. But I was stubborn, I wouldn't admit to taking it, much less give it up. I just refused to tell him. He pounded me for hours. "Where is it?" he demanded. "What have you done with my money?" He looked everywhere, but he couldn't find it. I was shaking, but trying not to show it. I didn't want to give myself away.

Then he shifted his tactics. He said, "Look, just put the money back and I'll leave you alone. But I'm going to pound you all day until that fifty shows up." And he kept his word. I let him beat me for a long time. I know I was giving away a lot of secrets to him by allowing him to beat me like that. I was letting him know how long he could pound me before I gave in. And it was a hell of a long time. Then he offered me another out. "Maybe I dropped it somewhere," he said. "I must have dropped it. If I find it I'll leave you alone. I'll stop." In other words, he was planting the seed in my head. I could pretend that I found the fifty by accident and put it back; and if I did that, I'd be off the hook.

I knew I'd gone too far. How I wished it had been just a five. I gave the money back to him a few hours later, but he didn't say, "Okay, forget it, you gave it back to me." No, he beat me up again, worse than the first time. He'd never had any intention of keeping his word. But still, in spite of the severe beatings, I felt like I had won, just a little bit. I had defied him, and it felt good. It was the same feeling I had when I went into the woods. I was desperate for a little bit of freedom, and, even as a child, I'd risk any punishment in order to get it.

Now that I knew the date my parents had been charged, I went back to the library. I felt like I was in a race to find the answers, and if I didn't hurry I'd miss them. I asked for the microfilm for the *Lawrence Eagle-Tribune* for 1961, but as soon as I had the January 1 issue on the screen, I hesitated. I took a deep breath and, gathering my courage, brought up the *Eagle-Tribune* for August 29, 1961.

It was on the back page.

The headline was "Case Continued." Nothing dramatic. The names of my mother and father—Carl and Ruth Theodore—leaped out at me. And then I picked up on the phrase "neglect of children." *Neglect of children*. That included me. I felt tears come to my eyes. I was unprepared for the intensity of my feelings.

Until that moment I'd been in denial. I was living in a dream world. I knew that the life I'd had was bad. I knew I was very depressed. I knew that I didn't want to be the way I was. But I'd never done anything about it, because I didn't want to face the reality.

Now, seeing my parents' names in print for the first time, I suddenly had a past, whether I wanted one or not. That article opened the floodgates. But it wasn't the article alone. It was the whole paper—the ads for Sunbeam bread, the way people were dressed in the photos.

That's how people lived back then. That's my past.

Seeing it on a screen was almost like watching a show on TV. *The Theodore Show.*

I had believed no one was stronger than my father, no one could whip him in a fight, no one was smarter. No one could put one over on him—

that was how I'd been taught to see him. Because he'd dominated and manipulated us all those years, it was hard for me to come to terms with the fact that he was really a very weak human being.

And, of course, I believed my mother was a saint.

If this wasn't true, I needed to see their names in black and white, in an article that said they were criminals for what they'd done to us. I needed to see it to come to terms with the idea that my parents—these people I'd idolized—*weren't good*. I felt betrayed and cheated. It was okay when I didn't know any different, but when I realized what I'd lost, I knew I had to do something to change. If you're in denial, you don't see that anything is wrong, so how do you turn it around?

I was like a zombie. One moment nothing was there, now the flood-gates had opened and I realized that my whole life up until then had been a fraud, like a magic trick—what do you call it?—a sleight of hand.

I knew there was more, that this article was only the tip of the iceberg. I had no idea what my brothers and sisters would think when they found out what I'd discovered, but I knew they weren't going to like it. They were all in denial, just as I had been.

I was the only one who wanted to dig into the past, and I was aware that the information I was certain to find would devastate me. But I also sensed that this search would put me on the path to healing myself. And once I was on that path, maybe I could go on to help heal my brothers and sisters, as well.

Now that I'd seen the newspaper article with my own eyes, I had the confirmation I needed. I felt like pinching myself. My parents are *criminals*. It was almost as if I didn't believe that it was really *them*. I had to say it out loud. I had to say it over and over again because I couldn't quite grasp the reality of it. They'd been arrested; they'd broken the law. What they'd done to me and my brothers and sisters was a crime.

I'd been right all along. I'd had my suspicions, but until now I never knew for sure. I'd wake up in the middle of the night in a sweat sometimes, and just lie there, trying to piece together what had happened to me—to all of us—as a kid. Did my father actually *do* that? Did they leave us alone for days at a time, with nothing to eat? I could never make up my mind whether I'd deserved to be punished for being a bad boy. The weird thing was that I never really thought before this that they were guilty of anything. But they *were* guilty. They were guilty as hell. And now I had the proof in my hands, proof that I'd been looking for but had never expected to find.

I couldn't hide from the truth anymore. I could no longer tell myself that, in spite of everything, my parents still loved me. *They didn't love me.* For the first time in my life, I was forced to step out of my denial and face the truth about my life head-on.

But I wasn't angry. My heart started to bleed. I was in excruciating pain, and I knew I had to do something.

I wanted to go right over to the District Attorney's office and file charges against them. I didn't care that it happened years ago. They'd committed a crime against us and been arrested and tried for it, but then they'd gone right back and done it again—and again. It wasn't as if they ever acknowledged that they'd made a mistake and learned from it. They were true criminals, not because of what they'd done once, but because of what they'd done again and again. I wanted to say to the district attorney, "Look, you arrested them. And you let them go and they did it again. And so you're partly responsible for what's happened to us."

Who was this man, my father, to treat us the way he had? What gave him the right to do what he did to us?

It had finally sunk in that I'd been abused. I felt sad and empty as I walked out of the courthouse. I should have been pleased that my search hadn't been in vain. Hadn't I gotten what I'd come for? Wasn't I now in a position to finally know why I'd suffered as a child, and why I was suffering now? But now that I had the key to the truth, I didn't know whether I could really handle it. I wasn't prepared for it. I might have been less shocked if I'd read that my parents were arrested for robbing a bank. That would have been bad, but if we'd had their love, I could have forgiven them. But they were criminals because of what they'd *done to us.* That's what made it so horrifying. We hadn't just imagined we were tormented. They'd been put in jail because the legal system said that they'd abused us.

I couldn't get over how much I'd lost, how much had been taken away from me so many years ago. But this was only the beginning of a long journey.

Poor was normal in Methuen. It was—and is still—just a humble little blue-collar town, where the richest people build things or have a little mom-and-pop store. But we were the poorest; we were at the bottom of the heap. I didn't have to look any further for proof of this than my memories of school.

At school, you get picked on if you're different. Kids don't really know any better. Well, from the beginning, all we Theodore kids were major targets. It got really bad when word got out that we had some kind of bug. It was probably true; I'm thinking it was head lice. The school gave us a special soap for it. That's when the kids said we had "Theodore germs." Every day in line for the playground, I'd get pushed and shoved by the aggressive kids, and the others would just move away from me. Kids ran off when they saw me coming, shouting, "Don't go near him, he's got cooties!" Or else they'd pinch their nostrils shut and say that I smelled. If I ever got close to anyone they'd slip out of line and go back to the end.

The aggressive kids didn't stop with shoving. I got whacks on the back of my head and punches to my shoulder and jaw. I tried—hard—to ignore all of it. I pretended I didn't care. But really they were hammering-in the same message I got at home every day: I, scrawny little Wayne Theodore, was worthless. And back then, I really believed that.

Since we were babies my father had taught me and my siblings that we were stupid and wouldn't get anywhere in this world. Now that I think about it, that was probably what he thought of himself. Anyway, once that thought was out there, there was nothing weird about being treated as worthless by other people, especially people our own ages. Our father also made sure we knew that people in the outside world were evil creeps who weren't to be trusted. We were trained to fear the outside so we wouldn't tell other people what was happening to us. He needed to control us. That was why we never had any friends. No one wanted to be our friends, anyway, but also we couldn't trust outsiders to be our friends. That partly explains why for so many years none of us ever thought of running away. Where would we go? The world our father had imprisoned us in was the only world we knew. Outside, we were told, it was far worse. Who would help us? They would only shun us and hurt us. We believed we were better off staying where we were.

The teachers didn't like us, either. Imagine what it feels like to have a teacher stand in front of the whole class and say to you, "Don't come to school tomorrow in those filthy clothes." It happened to all of us. A note would go home, and we'd get a beating because we'd done something that called attention to the family. And then we'd get a different dirty shirt and pair of pants from the pile in the bathroom to wear the next day.

The insults started first thing in the morning, on our way to school, and followed us right through the day. The abuse was constant—especially from the clique of older boys who always walked to school together. They made sure we knew we were the outcasts. We didn't belong anywhere. Sometimes they'd be hanging out playing on the way to school. As soon as they saw one of us coming, they'd stop what they were doing and call out, "Hey, what the hell are you looking at, Stinky Theodore, you smelly thing?" It was always Stinky or Smelly.

We were picked on pretty badly. All of us. My younger brother Michael got it the worst, because he was a very passive, timid kid and he kept to himself a lot. They decided there must be something wrong with him. "Michael's mental," they'd yell. The bigger kids in particular used to pick on him, and they'd single him out for a special type of humiliation. Because he sang to himself a lot, he became the object of ridicule. "Hey, Michael, whaddya say? Why don't you sing us a song? Sing something nice for us." And then they'd grab him and force him to sing. And while he was trying to please them so they wouldn't hurt him, they'd all stand around laughing and imitating him. There was no pleasing them. The next day they'd make him do it all over again.

They didn't stop at insults. There was a fair amount of swinging going on, too—punches to the chest, to the stomach, a sudden punch to the kidney. When we turned to see where an attack was coming from, we'd find two, maybe three or four, kids standing there. "What are you going to do about it, Stinky Theodore? You want a fight, asshole?" We knew if we tried to get back at them we'd get hurt, so we kept to ourselves as much as we could—not only because we didn't want to provoke the older kids. We had our orders. Our father told us every day when we went off to school not to talk to anyone else. There'd be hell to pay if we talked to outsiders. So we talked just to each other.

Like animals, we were marked because of the way we looked and smelled. But the worst part was, we didn't even know why.

I noticed that the other kids talked all the time. They'd say anything that popped into their heads. They were always laughing and gossiping, while we were all very quiet and withdrawn. When I looked at the older girls in fifth and sixth grades who all wore short skirts, I wondered why their legs didn't have any scars or bruises.

All kids were treated the way we were, I thought; they're just rich enough to be able to hide their marks. That was how I reasoned. The abusive situation wouldn't change just because you were a millionaire; that part was normal. They just hid it better. If we were rich, we might have better clothes and more to eat, but otherwise it would be just the same. Rich or poor, all children were beaten and abused.

That's just the way it is, I thought.

The hunger was there all the time. In the mornings I'd watch my schoolmates come into class carrying brightly colored lunchboxes. Then they'd put them on a shelf in the coat closet. I couldn't get my mind off them. What treasures were inside those lunchboxes? It was worse at lunchtime, when I actually saw what those millionaires' moms had given them. I'd be eating my ketchup or peanut butter sandwich on moldy pig bread, while the kids all around me were wolfing down bologna, cheese, ham, and turkey sandwiches. And their desserts! I couldn't believe all the cakes and Twinkies. I couldn't stop thinking about the Twinkies.

One day I got into trouble for some reason, and Mrs. Cole kept me in the classroom instead of allowing me out for morning recess. As I was sitting at my desk in the empty classroom, I began to think about all the food in those lunchboxes.

It took me a long time to work up the nerve to do it, but if I could pull it off, the payoff could be huge. Morning recess was my only chance. So I got myself in trouble again, only this time on purpose. I talked in class. Mrs. Cole made me stay in the classroom at recess. She went outside with the class and left me alone. As soon as everyone was gone, I sneaked back into the closet. At first all I did was peek inside the lunchboxes. Recess lasted only half an hour, so I didn't have long to choose what I wanted and then eat whatever I took. The first day I just took a cake. It was the most delicious cake in the world. When I saw that I could get away with it, I did the same thing again: I got in trouble by talking in class.

The next day I grabbed more: chocolate chip and oatmeal cookies and devil dogs. I never took a sandwich or a banana or apple. I didn't want it to look as though anything had been taken. Besides, most of the kids didn't know what they had in their lunchboxes in the first place.

This went on for a couple of weeks. It made it easier for me at lunch, when all these kids were eating their bologna and ham sandwiches, to know that I'd helped myself to some of their desserts. I didn't feel so ashamed eating my ketchup sandwich then.

One morning, while I was busy scavenging through the lunchboxes, the closet light suddenly flicked on and I looked up to see Mrs. Cole looming over me. She'd set me up. Instead of going out with the class to recess she'd stayed behind, lingering right outside of the classroom in the hallway.

She came over and twisted my arm really hard, wrenching it out of a lunchbox. "Wayne," she said sternly, "What are you doing?"

Well, she could see very well what I was doing. I tried to think up some excuse but there was nothing I could say. She gave me a lecture. That was to be expected. But then she sent a letter home with me to inform my parents of what I'd done. Naturally, I was severely beaten for exposing my father to the outside world.

It was agony in the schoolyard for two or three days after I was caught. The teacher shamed me for stealing. The kids shamed me because I was poor. "Don't you have any food at home?" they'd shout. "Hey, Theodore, what are you, poor? Why don't you eat your own food?" They wouldn't stop. They really had something on me this time, and they were mean.

I was hungry. I still couldn't get my mind off what was inside all those lunchboxes. I'd close my eyes and imagine biting into those Twinkies, those Hostess Cupcakes, those chocolate-chip cookies. In a way, it was worse than before, because I'd had them in my hands, and then they were taken away.

With a photocopy of the newspaper article about my parents' 1961 case in hand, I went back to the county courthouse. I saw the clerk who'd been so helpful to me before. I went up to her and showed her the article. I sensed that gradually I was winning her over. Now that she was taking an interest in my situation, I was hopeful she'd provide me with more information.

Sure enough, after a moment's hesitation, she said, "Have you ever heard of the Massachusetts Society for the Prevention of Cruelty to Children?"

This made me feel strange. "Wow," I said. "Is there actually such a thing?"

She explained that the Society not only existed, but it actually had investigated the case involving my parents. "In fact," she said, "we have a report from them about your parents on file."

This was far more than I'd expected. Seeing that article in the library was vindication enough for me, but now I was finding out there was a lot more. "Can I get a look at it?" I asked.

No, she said, she wasn't permitted to give it to me. Then she said, "But I'll tell you what, you can talk to the probation officer who handled the case."

This was astounding news. "You mean that guy is still alive?"

"Well, we're talking about 1961, not the Dark Ages," she said. "It wasn't that long ago." Then she got on the phone and called him. After a brief conversation she told me that he would see me now. His office was in another part of the building.

I was still in shock when the probation officer, an average-looking man in his mid-fifties, came out to greet me. He had a file in his hand. The sight of it gave me a strange feeling. *What's in it?* I wondered. *What long-buried secrets might it reveal?*

He motioned for me to sit. Then he opened the file and placed it on the desk between us without looking at it. It seemed he was already familiar with what it said.

"I remember this case very well," he began. He said that even after more than thirty years, he could still picture my parents clearly in his mind. "It was a very bad case," he said, "one of the worst in this state." Then he picked up the file and said, "I wish I could give this to you, but I can't."

Yet all I had to do was lean over a little bit and I was able to read the top page. I figured that he was trying to show it to me without being obvious. I had to fight back the temptation to grab it and bolt from the room. If I did that, though, I knew I'd be closing the doors on the past just when I was beginning to open them. Possibly because he remembered the case so well, the probation officer seemed fairly sympathetic to my plight. Even if he couldn't release the files he had, he said I had the option of going directly to the Massachusetts Society for the Prevention of Cruelty to Children—MSPCC, as he called it—or checking out the records in the State Department of Public Welfare.

"I recall that the State did an intake study on your family," he said. "So you might be able to get hold of that, too."

That was all the encouragement I needed. I was ready to begin my own personal excavation into the past, digging up whatever I could. I didn't care how much time it took me or how many bureaucrats I had to befriend. I was determined to uncover the truth from wherever it had been hiding all these years.

My search next led me to the State Department of Human Services. I found myself sitting across from a young woman who had what I wanted: She held the file on my parents' case in her hand. She was all smiles, but I could see she was trying to put me off. She gave me one excuse after another for why it might not be a good idea for me to see them. But from everything she was telling me, I gathered there was no law against her letting me have the file. I kept insisting. Finally, a little exasperated, she capitulated.

"To be honest with you, Mr. Theodore," she said, "if it were up to me I'd rather not give this to you. But I can't stop you. According to agency guidelines, you're entitled to see it." She cautioned me, though. "I think it would be best if you have someone with you when you read the report—maybe a therapist or a counselor. There's a lot in here that you're going to find very painful."

"I know someone I can ask. No problem," I lied. I was certain I could handle it on my own. Anyway, I'd say anything to get that report.

She gave me a dubious look, and then with a sigh she handed me the file, adding that several names in the report had been blacked out to protect people's privacy. Thanking her, I hurried out of her office. My hands were shaking. *Finally,* I thought, *I'm going to know the truth.* I didn't even wait until I got home. As soon as I climbed into my truck, I tore the envelope open. Then I began to read.

My father expected my mother to tell him everything we kids did. Every night when he came home, she had to fill him in on what trouble we'd gotten into. And if she told him none of us had done anything wrong—that we'd all been good kids—he'd tear into her and accuse her of lying. Sometimes, for my father's approval, John or another one of my brothers would say, "Dad, do you know what happened? Wayne left the yard today." Then my father would turn to my mother and say, "What the hell's wrong with you, why didn't you tell me Wayne did that?" My mother would stammer and say, "Well, I forgot to tell you," or she'd claim that she didn't know about it. My father would fly into a rage and beat her up.

She got into trouble with my father for other reasons, too. He'd decide the house wasn't clean enough, for instance. He'd go on about it for hours. It was torment having to listen to him fight with her. To avoid a beating, Ma would toil, sweeping and dusting like mad. I began to realize that, aside from doing laundry, she actually liked cleaning. It gave her something to do; it kept her mind off the horror of her life. Her cleaning sprees could last for weeks; then, with no warning, she'd fall into depression, and she wouldn't so much as look at a broom. That made my father crazy. She'd shrug and say, "Carl, I don't have enough soap." Stupid things like that.

My father would have liked to do with my mother what he did to his daughters and drag her around the house by her hair. He would gladly have "derooted" her, but he couldn't drag her far, because she was too big. Instead he kicked her while she lay on the floor. He called her names. He punched her in the face and in the stomach. He kicked her in her breasts.

"Why can't you do anything right?" he'd holler.

Once she made something she called "Greek soup" of hamburger meat, tomatoes, and noodles. My father said his mother used to make it, so he expected it to taste a certain way. I watched all this from just outside the kitchen doorway.

As soon as he put the spoon to his lips he made a face. "What the hell is this shit?" he said. Then he dumped the whole pan on the floor and started pounding her. He pulled her hair and kicked her, calling her names. Somehow she managed to get up off the floor and grab a knife off the counter. Then she retreated to the corner. She was shaking, barely able to hold the knife.

"I've had enough, Carl," she said, "I'm going to kill you, I swear I will!" Then she changed her mind and threatened to leave him—this time for good.

I'd seen them fighting many times before, but I'd never seen Ma pull out a knife like that. My heart was in my throat. Anything could happen in a flash. I thought, *I should do something, but what?* I was only twelve, and too small to help. Could I save Ma? Could I save myself? Maybe I should run. But I was frozen. I didn't want to look at what happened next, but I couldn't help it. My father didn't realize I was there. He was so mad at Ma he wasn't aware of anything else.

He lunged for her. Twisting her hand, he grabbed the knife away. She didn't put up any resistance. She just sat there, cowering and whimpering, waiting for the blows to come. I didn't want to see him win, but I was relieved to see that he wasn't about to kill my mother.

All at once my father looked down at the spilled soup and called out for Susan and Sheila. "Girls," he said, "clean this mess up. I want it cleaned up now."

The girls couldn't have been happier. They were doing something he wanted and that gave them comfort. If they were cleaning up his mess, they weren't being beaten. It was weird, being grateful to do some little job for him because it meant that, for the moment, anyway, you weren't in danger. It was a feeling I knew very well.

One night, not long after the soup incident, I woke up to the sound of my parents shouting and cursing. It had happened before, but this time I wanted to see what was going on. I crawled out of my bed. Some of my brothers and sisters followed. When I got to the hallway, I caught a glimpse of my mother standing in the corner near the bathroom with a kitchen knife in her hand. She was quivering and crying. I couldn't tell whether she was trying to scare him or make him think that she was going to kill herself. We watched the whole thing like it was a movie. He knew we were there, but it didn't matter to him. We had no significance, as far as he was concerned. And then he beat her up even with her holding the knife in her hand. He paid no attention to it; she didn't dare try to stab him. She just kept holding onto it. It was torture. She wouldn't give up easily. They fought until about midnight, and then he grew tired.

"Let's just go to bed," he said. And they went to bed as if nothing had happened.

Then we heard him fooling around with her. My mother kept saying, "No, stop it, Carl, stop it," and my father kept saying, "You're nothing but a whore, now roll over."

I was too young to know then what it meant, but now I know that he was essentially raping her.

And this happened for years—the threats, the fights, and the rapes.

S itting in my pickup truck outside the Department of Human Services I tore open the envelope and started to read. It is so eerie, seeing your family described, in black and white, through the eyes of a complete stranger. It's a little like looking the wrong way through a telescope.

The report described my father as "a 29-year-old short, muscular man . . . constantly seeking security through material possessions. . . . He seeks tangible evidence of status, buying tractors, trucks, and horses to fill this need, generally losing money when he sells them. This has been a major source of conflict between the parents and has deprived the children of physical needs. His understanding of either the physical or emotional needs of children is nil."

And this was what the report said about my mother: "She is a 23-year-old, short, heavy, depressed woman who often appears rather childlike, both in facial expressions and the ideas and hopes she expresses. She has a great verbalized need to be loved, this stemming from the deprivation she experienced as a child. She spent most of her childhood with maternal great-grandparents. . . ."

The report describes how she'd run away, and then always come back: "Although she intellectually admits that she would be better off without the father, her drive to be loved forces her to return to him after each desertion, against familial advice. At the same time, she claimed that she'd been unwanted even as a child and said that her own past difficulties have made her more aware of her children's needs for love. She has used the children to rationalize why she has returned to live with the father."

Here is an account of what one of these social workers found when she came to call not long after my parents had reconciled:

"The mother was barefoot. The children were also barefooted. They all had one pair of shoes, but they didn't fit and the father wouldn't buy them new ones because they weren't worn out. In the kitchen there was a stove, a chrome table, and four chairs. In one bedroom there was a crib and a bureau; in another a single bed and in the front room a table, bed, TV, and maple arm chair for the father and a kitchen chair for the mother. There was only one toy for the children to play with in the house. Two children sleep in each bed. There was no high chair, carriage, or playpen. The house was spotlessly clean."

Looking back on it, I suppose the reason the house was so clean was because my parents were expecting a visit from a social worker. My father must have laid down the law to Ma and told her that if the social worker found a speck of dust he'd make her pay for it.

When the social worker asked my mother about her marriage this was the response she received:

> Mrs. Theodore stated with pride that her husband had left a list of the work she was to do that day, and she had finished it. She was very limited in intelligence. It is doubtful that her husband understands this, and only at times realizes that she must constantly be supervised. She stated that he was a very good father, and when the worker asked if he assumed any care of the children, she stated 'no.' When he comes home at night, she washes and changes his clothes, and also serves him his dinner. She then serves the children their dinner. He goes in to watch television and she puts the children to bed. He does not help with the children in any way. She informed the worker that she would like to have another baby.

It would be funny if it weren't my life.

So those were my parents: a father who had no understanding of either the emotional or physical needs of his children and a depressed, unloved mother who not only kept returning to a man who brutalized her, but who wanted to have more children with him.

The beatings didn't stop even when my mother was pregnant. My father had no compunction about beating her when her belly was huge. He'd kick her in the gut. He used to say it, too, so she'd know what was coming. "I'll kick you in the gut, Ruth. Double you over." And he'd do it. She had at least four miscarriages, maybe five. So you'd have to say along with everything else my father's done that he's committed murder.

One day, after he'd beaten her mercilessly, she ran into the bathroom and sat on the toilet for the longest time. I was only seven years old, but already I'd seen this happen before, where she'd closet herself in the bathroom. But until now I never had a chance to find out what she was doing in there. She came out looking pale and shaken and muttered something to the effect that her baby was in the toilet. I wanted to see it. I wanted to see what it looked like. This was one of those times when there wasn't any water to flush the toilet. We snuck into the bathroom—there were four or five of us—to have a look. It was just a big glob of blood and tissue, a brother or sister I would never have.

The morning after my mother lost the baby, I woke up and sensed that something had changed. My mother seemed strangely calm, as if she had something big on her mind, like she was bursting with a secret she was dying to reveal. My father was in a weird mood, too. He was almost civil toward her. He probably knew he'd gone too far the night before. The minute she heard him get into the car she went to the window and peeked out. She waited until she was sure he was gone, and then she went straight to the closet. We stood there in amazement, wondering what she was doing. Then she began pulling out tattered old suitcases and garbage bags.

"Come on, kids," she called to us. "We've got to pack. Put all your stuff in these bags and let's get out of here."

We'd left home before, but this time my mother instructed us to take more clothes with us. "I'm never coming back here," she declared. And I believed her. I was actually convinced. The feeling was really powerful. Just the thought of not having him around anymore or being beaten up by him made me happy.

An hour later we were marching down the highway, a ragtag army of little snotty-looking, ratty kids, the big ones carrying the bags and the smaller ones trailing behind, led by a fat woman with a crying baby in her arms. Half of us didn't even have any shoes on! What a sight we must have been. People would just sort of stop and gape at us. Motorists would slow down just to get a better look.

We had no idea where we were going and she wouldn't tell us. But who cared? We were just anxious to make our escape. My mother urged us to hurry up and walk faster. We walked and walked. I'd never been so far from home before, and the whole time I was marching down the highway I could feel the freedom in every step. *We're getting away. We're leaving him. We're going to be free.* So it didn't really matter where my mother was taking us. The only thing that counted was that we were free of my father. It was a strange feeling, but it was a good feeling.

By about midday, it was getting hot and we were all sweating. We were bone-tired, and our legs hurt so much we could barely keep them moving. But no one wanted to stop. Suppose my father decided to come home from work early? He'd probably drive by and see us. Then we'd be in for it. We knew that any dallying, any stopping to rest, would be too dangerous.

We continued a little farther, and were getting into unknown territory. This was a big journey we were going on. All of a sudden, I spotted the bridge that ran over the Merrimack River. This was the same bridge I could see from the top of our hill, watching the cars come and go. It was strange to see it so close, when once it seemed a thousand miles away.

After a while we began to see shops and taller buildings. My mother told us that we were coming into Haverhill. I'd seen it from a car but never like this. This was our destination. Haverhill sounded like freedom to me.

My mother led us up one street and down another. Finally we came to a gray clapboard house. Ma walked up to the door and rang the bell. When the door opened, her grandmother appeared. I recognized her, although it had been years since I'd seen her. They hadn't come to visit us for years, because they were afraid of my father and had always disapproved of my mother marrying him. I later found out that, many years before, my grandmother had more or less disowned her daughter for hanging around bars and fooling around with men. I guess when my great-grandmother saw us all standing there she must have taken pity on us. She motioned to us and told us to come in. Then she called to my great-grandfather to let him know of our arrival.

We were given a warm welcome—that was unusual for us—but you could tell we weren't expected. They kept looking us over because they hadn't seen us for so long. Of course, they were surprised to see how big we'd gotten, but we got the same reaction from them that we always got from people outside the family—shock. They didn't say anything about it, not in front of us anyway, but I could see by the look in their eyes that they were upset by how dirty we looked, and battered and bruised.

My mother kept assuring us that we were safe with her and had nothing to worry about. All the same, I wondered. I guess I had a little bit of an empty feeling, too. What are we going to do now? Where are we going to live? We couldn't stay at my grandparents' house forever. Besides, my father would be looking for us, and sooner or later (probably sooner) he'd find us. My mother was pretty predictable when it came to running. What's more, my father had grown up in Haverhill; he knew the territory. When my mother ran, the first place she'd go was her grandparents' house. So naturally that would be the first place he'd look.

That meant it was just a matter of time before he showed up. We lived in dread. Every time a car door slammed in front of the house our hearts would pound and we'd look for someplace to hide. There were a lot of false alarms.

Then, one night, while we were in the living room watching TV, we heard the bell ring. We all looked at each other. We froze, too scared to move. My great-grandfather went to the door. It was my father.

My great-grandfather didn't let him in. He stood in the doorway and told my father to go away. "If you don't leave we're going to call the police," he said. Then he shut the door in his face.

My father refused to leave. He stood outside the door for an hour. "Just let me talk to her," he said forlornly. "Ruth, just let me talk to you. Please, Ruth, I've got to talk to you." He was begging. He felt that if he could get her outside to talk then he'd be able to convince her to come back. I could see the doubt creeping into my mother's eyes, like maybe she should hear what he had to say, but my great-grandfather would have none of it. He was furious by this point, and he went to the door again and shouted, "Carl, I meant what I said. I'm telling you for the last time. If you don't get the hell off my property I'm going to call the cops."

We were all sitting there, trembling like scared rabbits, because we knew what my father was capable of. We were petrified that he was going to break down the door and scoop us up one by one and take us back to Methuen with him.

To our relief, he finally gave up and drove off. But we weren't reassured. We knew he'd be back.

My father wouldn't leave us alone. He kept stopping by. "I love my kids," he'd say. "Ruth, let me *see* the kids, at least." Eventually she relented, and let Michael and me see him. He'd drive around the block with us a few times and ask us questions—mostly about my mother.

"So," he'd say, "what's up with your mom? Who's she seeing? Who does she talk to? Where does she go during the days?"

He kept probing us about what my mother had planned for us. Where were we going to live? he asked. And then he'd say, very casually, as if the thought had only just occurred to him, "So, kids, do you think you want to come home?"

Then, one day, to my amazement, he began to cry. I'd never seen anything like it before. I looked at Michael. He looked at me. He was just as astounded as I was—and bewildered, too.

"You don't know how much I miss you all," my father went on. "It's so lonely without you kids. The house feels so empty."

We really felt bad for him. Michael and I were thinking the same thing: He really likes us. We'd never believed it before, but it was what we'd wanted all along. Could he finally have woken up to what he'd been doing to us? I desperately hoped—we all hoped—that he'd changed. We wanted to believe it, but how could we know for certain?

My father's visits became a regular occurrence. He told us life would be different if we came back. We'd get all the attention if we came back, he promised, because it was just going to be him and us. My mother could stay in Haverhill if she wanted to, but we'd go back to Methuen. That was a very big thing.

Still, I could tell he wasn't a hundred percent sincere. He wanted us to think he'd changed, and we really hoped he had, but experience taught me to be wary. I was still suspicious.

Sometimes when my father came to see us, he drove us past the Schwinn bicycle store. He deliberately parked right in front of the store so I could feast my eyes on the bikes in the window. He asked me what I thought of them. He could see I wanted one. He was holding out the promise of buying me one if I agreed to move back in with him.

"Don't you want to come home and live with Dad? It'll be good. It'll be a lot of fun. I'll give you a bike of your very own. Wouldn't you like that?" He guaranteed every one of his boys a new bike—Mike would get one, so would Joseph. John, because he was too small for a regular bike, would get a mini-bike. We'd all luck out—that was his story.

Then he stopped at a grocery store and bought a little bag of candy and gave it to us. "You guys are good kids," he said. "You deserve this." We believed every word of it. He was a champion. It was hard to resist all the attention he was lavishing on us. Nothing like this had ever happened before. It got so we actually wanted to go back with him. This time it would be different, we thought. It actually sounded as if he were going to reform. We really began to believe him.

Meanwhile my mother was planning our future, too, only it was a different future from the one my father had in mind. About three weeks had gone by since we'd moved to Haverhill. It was time to get a place of our own, my mother said. So she'd rented a place in town just down the hill from where my grandparents lived.

"Whatever you do, Wayne—Michael are you listening?—don't tell your dad about it," she warned.

Our new home turned out to be an apartment in a dingy three-floor tenement building in a rundown area of Haverhill. Six families lived in the building. My mother told us she was never going back to Methuen and that moving into this apartment was proof of that. She said she'd get a job and support us somehow. But instead of being happy, we were disappointed. We'd expected her to say she'd decided to return to Methuen, after all. Our father wanted us back. Couldn't she see that?

My father was relentless. When he wanted something, he wouldn't give up. He kept coming back to visit with us and buying us candy and plying us with promises of the good life we'd have if we lived with him.

Sometimes I believed my father had changed, but if he hadn't, then there was only one reason he kept coming around: He wanted us to keep an eye on our mother for him, and he was counting on us to work on her. He would use us to reach her.

He was right. We'd kind of gang up on her. "Come on, Ma," we'd say. "We should go home. Let's go home." After a while all that pressure got to her.

At the same time, though, my father continued to offer us his alternative scenario. Some of us could go and live with him and our mother could stay where she was. It was so appealing; he seemed so loving, and that was what I'd always wanted, for my dad to love me the way other dads love their kids. I knew I had to give it a chance.

As it turned out, my brothers felt the same way. So we agreed to go home with him—Joseph, Michael, John, and me. My sisters would stay with Ma in Haverhill.

It had been a month since we'd been home. Once we stepped inside our house, the bad memories came flooding back.

For one thing, I could see that nothing had changed; the place was still a dump—worse now, because my mother hadn't been there to clean.

The first night back I woke up with a feeling of terror. Nothing bad had happened, but I had a weird feeling in my gut. Even though I was only a child, I had strong gut feelings, and I usually paid attention to them. I began to be afraid. Maybe I'd made a mistake, I thought. Maybe I'd have been better off in Haverhill. No matter what my father had promised us, now that we were alone with him, I couldn't help thinking that at any moment the old Carl Theodore was going to return and beat the hell out of me.

At first, my father was on his best behavior, though I could see it was a real strain on him. We spent the first two days with him, and the whole time my brothers fought for his attention. Hadn't he told us we were all going to get new bikes and everything? So now they competed to see who was going to get the most out of this new dad of ours.

I didn't compete so much with my brothers. Instead, I kind of hung back, because I had that sense that deep-down, in spite of everything he'd promised me, he still hated my guts. At the same time I thought that it would be better if my mother stayed put in Haverhill and didn't come back. If we had him alone, we might be able to handle him. I knew that life was always worse for me when my parents were together than when they were apart, but it would take me many years to discover why.

Over the next two days my father was away a lot. He'd be gone for hours. He didn't tell us what he was doing but it was obvious to us that he was going back to Haverhill to see our mother. He wasn't going to settle for only four of his kids.

Then, on the third day, I heard the car pull up in the driveway and a few moments later the front door opened and he walked in. My mother was right behind him with Christopher, the baby, in her arms. The minute I saw her walk in the door I said to myself, *The party's over.* And I knew it was over just by what he said. "Now that we're all back here, Ruth, don't think we're going to let these kids get away with murder. These kids are animals."

Minutes before, we'd been great kids. Now suddenly we were animals. He didn't say it in a mean way, but in a nice, almost offhanded way that made his words sound even more menacing.

Then he said something to my mother that made me shudder. "Gee," he said, "You know I don't want to hurt the kids or anything, but they've got to learn some discipline."

Got to learn some discipline. I knew what that meant.

And the most upsetting part about this whole conversation was that she was agreeing with him.

"You're right, Carl, the kids do need disciplining," she said. "I know we can't let them get away with murder, but things aren't going to be like they were before."

She didn't sound convinced, though.

If we dared to remind him about the bikes and the other things he'd promised, he'd deny everything.

"You're crazy," he'd say. "What are you talking about?"

He was punishing us—me especially—for having had to pretend to be nice to us. Now he had to get some payback, some retribution for being nice.

We didn't have to wait long. After a month or two, something snapped; my father couldn't hold it in anymore. We recognized the signs—the narrowing eyes, the pursed lips, the clenched fists. He'd stare at Ma as if he was trying to make up his mind whether to slap her around now or wait until later. She pretended that everything was going along okay, but she could sense what was coming.

He didn't need an excuse. A word, a funny look, a piece of furniture that wasn't dusted—anything could set him off. It was only a matter of time. But when the explosion finally happened, it was because of me. He'd grabbed me by the scruff of the neck and was ready to teach me a lesson—but what did I do? I don't remember—when my mother did something totally unexpected.

She actually spoke up. "Don't beat him up, Carl, don't touch him!" She still thought he might really have changed.

He looked at her as if he couldn't believe what he was hearing. "How can you say 'don't beat the kid up?'" Then the curses came flying out of his mouth. His hand, balled into a fist, sailed through the air and a second later Ma was on the floor, her jaw swollen and beet-red. The sight of her sprawled out only seemed to incite my father more. He began to kick her with his heel, the way he always did, slamming it against her chest.

Things were right back to the way they were before—exactly the same. For all the difference it had made in our lives, we might have never left home at all.

Delving deeper into the government file, I sat bolt upright when I came across the following letter:

September 8, 1961

Massachusetts Society for the Prevention of Cruelty to Children
Honorable John J. Darcy, Justice
Lawrence District Court

Dear Judge Darcy:
This is a report of our investigation according to the General Laws, Chapter 119, Section 24, into conditions affecting the Theodore children. The house owned and occupied by this family consists of four rooms, kitchen, and bath. The family moved to the home three years ago when only a shack was there, and the parents have been building and enlarging the house since then. This remarkable accomplishment came at the expense of the children's food and clothing. While the mother insists that she worked hard to maintain a clean home, she also admits that when she was "fed up" with the father's verbal and physical abuse, she would lose interest and allow the home to sink into deplorable filth. She complained of not having had hot water, mops, or much soap to keep the house clean enough. . . . Between 8–22–61 and 9–1–61, I was unable to locate the parents and gain admittance. I did observe that the outside of the home was somewhat neglected and

overgrown, that the entryway to the home was saturated with the smell of urine, and that every window of the house was completely covered, preventing any view of the interior. I also observed a four foot high barrel outside of the house filled with rotting, feces-encrusted children's clothes, which not only deprived the children of adequate clothes, but also presented a health hazard.

Between 8-22-61 and 9-1-61, I was unable to locate the parents. . . .

Had we been abandoned? Then I came to this description:

The present situation came to the attention of the Methuen Police Department and the MSPCC on 8-21-61 when they learned that on 8-19-61 the mother had left the father, following an argument about in-law interference, leaving the children in his care. In the course of the argument the father struck the mother. This was the third documented desertion of this calendar year. Following this desertion, the children were voluntarily placed in a Haverhill Children's Aid and Family Service foster home for a one week period.

I closed my eyes and let my mind drift into the past. I was three years old, peeking out the living room window through a tear in the plastic. Three strangers—all men—were walking up to the front door. Could that have been what the report was referring to? Was that the time my father left us all alone? Like a door swinging wide, my memory suddenly opened up.

We were alone in the house—six of us. My mother had disappeared again. And when it got dark that night, my father never came home.

The next day, the same thing happened. Where were our parents? We had no idea. When would they be back? We didn't know. Maybe never—and to a three-year-old, anything seemed possible.

We didn't have enough to eat. We were surviving on crab apples we plucked off the trees in the backyard. It wasn't enough to fill our stomachs: We were starving, and now we were also getting diarrhea. The house had only that one manual toilet, and it stank.

But that wasn't the worst part. We were scared. We'd been trained to be afraid of strangers, and so we were terrified of the three men who kept coming into the yard. We'd hear them before we saw them, crunching the grass underfoot. What were these men doing here, and why did they keep coming back? They'd knock at the door, and call to us, "Is anyone home?"

When I look back now, I know they must have heard us moving around. They must have known we were inside. We never answered. We were petrified. We'd run off in a corner and hide. That was how we'd been trained. We knew they couldn't see in because of plastic covering the windows. But there were rips in the plastic, so I peeked out, and some of my older siblings did, too.

Then one day they didn't walk away. This time they broke the door down and barged in. We all began to cry and scream and scamper for cover. The men were too fast for us, though, and they grabbed us one after another. They were telling us to calm down, but we didn't know who they were, and our first reaction was that they were there to hurt us. I thought that they were going to take us away from the house, and we'd never see our parents again. Our lives were filled with beatings, and we were terrified of anything out of the ordinary.

How could we have known that they were coming to save us?

W e'd been abandoned before. It was right there in the report from the state. "Our agency has a record of previous contact with the family, which describes the long standing deprivation to which these parents, as well as these children, have been subject."

Reading those words jogged yet another faint memory in my mind. I'd had flashes before, but I'd always believed I'd dreamed it. Maybe it did happen, after all. It would have been better if it had been a dream, a nightmare.

One day when I was three or four, my father said, "Joe and Bill are going to look after you kids while I'm gone." This was during one of those times when my mother had disappeared.

We looked up at our father when he said this, puzzled.

"They're good friends of mine." My father was trying to keep it light and casual.

But we weren't interested in Joe and Bill. We wanted to know why our father was leaving and how long he'd be gone. Now that we'd lost our mom, it looked like we were about to lose our father, too.

But he wouldn't tell us anything further. He just kept going on about how we should be good kids and not be a bother to Joe and Bill.

It was years before I found out that everyone called these two men "Nutty Joe" and "Crazy Bill." They deserved their names. Joe and Bill were scraggly drunks about my father's age. As soon as they walked into our house they acted like they owned the place. They looked mean, and they played mean pranks on us. They jabbed us with sharpened pencils just to see us jump. They jammed nails into our butts and laughed when we screamed. They tied us to trees and poked us with lit cigarettes.

"That's just a taste of what's coming if you do that again," they'd say.

They were always taunting my sister Susan, who was five or six years old.

"Come here, sweetheart." When she ran away, they said, "You hear what I just said? What's wrong with you? I gotta teach you to listen?"

When they caught her, they took turns fondling her. She had to bite her lips not to cry out. There was so much pain and fear in her eyes I almost couldn't bear to look at her, but I couldn't help myself. They stretched her out on the kitchen table. Undid the buttons on her dress. Ripped the cloth. Every time she squirmed to get away, they pinned her down harder.

"Where are you going, honey? You're not thinking of leaving us, are you, honey?"

Then they realized that they weren't alone.

"What are you looking at, you little creep?"

I ran off. But where did I think I was going? There weren't enough places in the house to hide. There was nowhere to hide in the whole world.

always hated Christmas. Everyone at school could talk of nothing else for weeks, but, for the Theodore kids, Christmas holidays were like a jail sentence.

I knew basically what Christmas was from what I'd seen on TV and what the other kids told me. I knew that Santa Claus was a big deal, but he was never going to come down our chimney, even if we got one. What was all this fuss about getting presents? We didn't have any money, anyway, so there were no presents coming to us. Just more beatings—that was what we expected from Christmas, because that's what we expected every other day.

For the other kids, Christmas meant a vacation from school, and everybody loved vacations—but we hated them. As bad as school was, it was a lot better than staying home. What made it worse was knowing that while we were getting beaten up all the other kids would be sitting around the Christmas tree, unwrapping their presents. Every time I thought about what was going on in other people's houses, my stomach clenched. And the question just would not go away: *Why?*

Growing up, I lived through a lot of bad Christmases. Since then, I've had good Christmases. But it's the Christmas I was ten that I'll never forget. On Christmas morning I'd woken up to find I'd wet my bed again. And I knew what that meant. A few minutes later, my face was being mashed into the Pine-Sol–urine bed. I had to keep my face pressed there for at least an hour. The combination of urine and Pine-Sol burned my cheeks and forehead. From time to time I'd lift my head up to take in a breath. I'd hear my father yell from the other room, "I hope you ain't taking your head out of the mattress," as if he knew what I was up to without having to watch me. After a while he decided I'd had my face in the urine-soaked bed long enough. He came in and grabbed me by the hair and dragged me out and started beating me again. Then he made me take off my wet pants, and he stuck them in my face and told me to stand in the corner, completely naked. It was late in the morning and I hadn't had a thing to eat. That's when I heard a knock on the door. That was a surprise. It was something that never happened.

My mother was as puzzled as I was. She hurried to look out the window to see who it was. I couldn't imagine. The only person I could think would trudge all the way up the road to see us was a bill collector. Bill collectors were chasing my father all the time. But it wasn't a bill collector. It was Uncle Albert and Aunt Betty and their two kids, a boy and a girl. The girl was probably a year or two younger than I was, and the boy was just a toddler. (He died of hepatitis C when he was nine or ten. No one ever knew how he got it.) They'd parked their car down at the gate and walked up the road.

Uncle Albert was my mother's half-brother, and my father tolerated him and Aunt Betty up to a point, because they kept their mouths shut. Besides, he always thought that Uncle Albert was a little bit soft in the head, so it made him feel superior. He was always downing Albert.

"He's okay," he'd say, "but I don't want him over here all the time."

And for the most part they knew enough to stay away; if they came over once a year it was a big deal. But Christmas was a special occasion, after all, so they just decided to show up out of nowhere. They'd brought some toys with them—a toy gun, some GI Joes, and a couple of matchbox cars, and a doll for one of my sisters. They didn't bring a toy for everyone, though, because it had been so long since they'd come to visit that they didn't know how many kids there were, all together.

I was so happy when I found out who it was. I thought, "Wow, somebody's here to save me."

I had blisters all over my face from the Pine-Sol, and fresh bruises from the beating. I was naked, and cowering in a corner. Even with urine-soaked pants in my face, I could see them staring at me. I tried looking anywhere else but I could still feel their eyes on me. My face burned with embarrassment. Maybe they thought it was red just from the beating. Every few minutes my father would remember I was there, and to show off to his guests he'd bash me over the head. But I could take the pain. The pain was nothing next to the humiliation.

Nobody said a word for a long time after my uncle and aunt walked in. Nobody asked, "Hey, what's he doing standing in the corner like that?" They just pretended to ignore me.

"He's Mr. Piss Pants in the corner," my father explained to my uncle. "He pissed all over the damn bed and all over the house. He's Mr. Piss Pants. He's a rotten bastard, and this is how he's going to learn."

Uncle Albert had no problem with it. He was looking at me like, "Yeah, okay, he got what he deserves." He seemed to agree with my father.

I had a feeling from the way she was looking at me that my Aunt Betty felt sorry for me. I had a feeling she wouldn't do it to her own kids, and that she disapproved.

What bothered me most, though, were their two kids, especially the girl. Here I was, standing there naked with urine-soaked pants in my face. She was around nine. I half-expected her to burst out laughing, but she didn't.

Then they started to act like I wasn't there, and they all sat around talking for ten or fifteen minutes. There really wasn't much to say. They could try to ignore me, but it was hard to do. I was the whole show. Then my father started to make them feel uncomfortable. He was good at that. He said, "We're going to have to go soon." We didn't have anywhere to go, it was just an excuse to get them out of the house, but my uncle and aunt took the hint.

"Okay," they said. "We won't keep you. We're on our way." I guess they were happy to go.

About an hour after they'd left, my father told me to drop the wet pants in the pile of dirty clothes and put some fresh clothes on and then go sit on the porch. I didn't have to stand in the corner anymore with my dirty pants in my face. That was my Christmas present.

One day in late January, when I was in the fifth grade, I managed to turn what was supposed to be a routine assignment into something else altogether. Instead of doing my homework, I decided to write a letter to my teacher, Miss Callahan. It was a nasty letter. I called her a slut, a whore, and a bitch. Every swear word that came into my head went on that piece of paper. I don't even know why I did it. By the time I was finished, I was full of rage. The strange thing was that I had no real reason to be angry with Miss Callahan—she wasn't my favorite teacher, but she was no worse than any of the other teachers I'd had. It was just that all this anger was festering in me and it came boiling out in the letter. *I'm going to get you, Miss Callahan.* That was what I was thinking. I even went ahead and signed the damn thing, so she wouldn't have any doubt about who'd written it.

After classes were over for the day I slipped up to her desk and placed the letter front and center, so she couldn't miss it. Then I thought to myself, *What am I doing? I could get killed—not by the teacher but by my father, once he finds out.* So I went back. The lights were off but I could still see the letter. Thank God. I picked it up and slipped out. I made sure to rip up the letter so no one would find it even accidentally.

A day later, though, I changed my mind again. I felt this overpowering urge to write another letter to Miss Callahan, an urge even stronger than the first one. I called her just about everything in the book.

"Dear Fat, Ugly Bitch," I wrote, "I hate you. You should be dead."

This time I didn't sign it.

It was as if I blamed her for every bad thing that was happening to me. But I didn't come right out and say I was being beaten up all the time. I didn't put in the letter what was going through my head the whole time I was writing it. I didn't say that I was desperate and wanted someone to help me.

The words I scribbled in the letter to her were the words I heard in my house every day. They were the words that my father said to my mother.

I told myself I wasn't going to chicken out. I folded the letter up and waited until Miss Callahan had her back to me. Then I slipped it onto her desk. I was feeling a little cocky, like I'd accomplished something major. But just as I was about to leave the school building, I began again to have second thoughts. Suddenly I became really scared of what might happen, especially the beatings I was sure to get, so I went back to the classroom. It was empty, and the lights were off, but I didn't need any light to see that the letter was gone. It was too late to do anything about it.

I was very nervous. *What did I just do?* I couldn't understand why I'd written the letter to begin with. It had seemed like the thing to do at the time, but now that Miss Callahan actually had the letter in her hands, it hit me that I might be in serious trouble. It really bothered me, because I'd made an enemy of Miss Callahan, and I'd done it without having any idea why.

I could picture her reading it. I could imagine the horror and shock in her face. Even though I hadn't signed it, she'd know who had written it. She'd have no trouble recognizing my handwriting.

Sure enough, the next day she came up to me in class and asked me if I'd written the letter. I could barely meet Miss Callahan's eyes. The other kids were looking at me, too, wondering what mischief I'd gotten myself into now.

I was right: She was more shocked than angry. And she was hurt, too. I could see it in her eyes. She didn't understand why I'd called her all those names. Her hand was trembling as she held out the letter. "Did you write this, Wayne?"

I nodded, keeping my eyes down.

"Why?"

I shrugged. How could I answer her when I didn't know myself?

"*Wayne.*"

The way she said my name made me want to crawl under my desk. I could only keep repeating that I didn't know why I'd written the letter.

There was nothing more to say. I didn't write it because I was angry. I didn't write it because Miss Callahan had made me do a hard assignment or had looked at me funny. It just seemed to have come out of me.

After a while she got tired of my shrugs and silences. She grabbed me by the arm and took me straight to the principal's office. That was pretty scary. I didn't want to have to face Mrs. Mulcahey. She was old-school, with frosted hair and a purple nose. She was a mean woman. I don't remember ever seeing a smile on her face the whole time I was at the Pleasant Valley School.

Mrs. Mulcahey told me to sit while she read the letter. Her face flushed. When she looked back up at me she asked me the same kinds of questions Miss Callahan had asked.

"What were you thinking when you wrote this, Wayne?" she asked. "I don't understand why you'd do something so terrible."

She stopped and looked at me, expecting me to offer some explanation, but I was too nervous to speak. I couldn't get out a word. I just sat there, feeling miserable.

She went on. "This sort of thing is intolerable. We won't stand for it. I'm going to have to talk to your parents."

Talk to my parents? I'd really done it this time. This was the worst punishment she could have given me.

She sent a letter home with my sister Susan, saying that she wanted my parents to come in the next day and have a talk with her.

Only my mother showed up. She wore the same baggy gray dress she always wore, and she looked quite put out. Obviously she didn't want to be there. She wasn't used to dealing with officials. I was told I had to attend the meeting, too. So I sat in the principal's office, staring at the floor, while my mother listened to Mrs. Mulcahey explain how her kid had badly misbehaved. I was squirming; I just wanted to get out of there.

"Mrs. Theodore, I don't know how to put this exactly," Mrs. Mulcahey said, "but I think Wayne may have a serious emotional problem. I think he needs help." She was looking directly at me. I didn't like the way she said "help."

"This school may not be appropriate for him," she went on. "He may belong somewhere where trained professionals can evaluate him."

My mother didn't know what to say. She mumbled something about how she was so busy with all her kids that she couldn't mind me the way she should. It was clear that she would say anything to be let off the hook and get out of there.

I knew what Mrs. Mulcahey was really saying. *This boy is retarded and we want to wash our hands of him.* She didn't think it had anything to do with problems at home. It was all I could do to keep myself from crying out that I wasn't retarded, that Mrs. Mulcahey had gotten it all wrong, but I didn't say a word. I was afraid that if I said anything I'd only make matters worse. Maybe they'd actually go ahead and put me in an institution. Michael, who was one year younger than I was, had already been placed in a special school because he had a learning disability. And my oldest brother, Joseph, had to take special classes. So it was almost as if we were already marked. They knew us. By writing the letter I'd made them think that I was just another dumb Theodore kid.

Then Mrs. Mulcahey announced that she was suspending me for three days until the end of the week. That was all the *school* was going to do to me, but I knew that severe beatings were coming. And it would be worse than usual, because it was the middle of winter and my father was home all the time, living off his unemployment checks. For the next three days, I was beaten from morning to night. As much as I dreaded walking back into Miss Callahan's classroom, I couldn't wait to get out of the house and back to school.

The beatings I got really had nothing directly to do with my writing the letter. My father was angry because I'd created an awkward situation for him. I'd put him in danger of being exposed. I'd brought unwanted attention to him from the school authorities. He hated that. Maybe, looking back on it, that's why I did it.

When my suspension was over, I knew I had to do something. I felt guilty about the letter. Finally I got up my nerve to apologize to Miss Callahan and tell her how sorry I was. No one had made me apologize. I just did it on my own, because I was trying to make up with her. I didn't want her to hate me.

Miss Callahan looked me up and down, like she was checking me out to see whether I was sincere. Then she said she accepted my apology, and she went back to work. I knew, though, that there was nothing I could say that would ever make things better between us. She was still going to hate me.

One day, later that same year, I was called down to the principal's office.

Uh-oh, I thought, *what did I do now?* I couldn't think of anything. Since getting caught for writing the letter, I'd been careful to stay out of trouble. If another note were sent home, there would be more beatings for getting the family noticed again by the school authorities. I became more and more scared as I walked downstairs to the first floor and made my way to the dreaded office at the end of the long hallway.

The secretary let me into Mrs. Mulcahey's office. When I walked in, I was shocked to see Joseph sitting there with his shirt up over his head. There were bruises and black-and-blue marks all the way down his back. I don't know where she'd learned that something might be the matter with him. A school nurse and a teacher were there with Mrs. Mulcahey and they were all examining his bruises. This was the first time that I knew of that the school nurse had taken any interest in us. Before I could figure out what was going on, Susan was brought into the office, too. We exchanged looks but we didn't say anything.

"How did he get these bruises?" Mrs. Mulcahey asked us.

I lowered my eyes the way we always did when we had to talk to a grown-up. I knew what I was supposed to say, though, and I did. "He fell out of a tree." I said.

"I'm going to ask you once more where those bruises came from," she said. "You don't have to be afraid. You can tell us the truth, because we'll protect you."

"I told you," Joseph said. "I fell out of a tree."

"How did this happen?" Mrs. Mulcahey said, turning to me again. Obviously she didn't believe us.

"Uh . . . he fell out of a tree," I stammered.

"That's right, that's what happened," Joseph chimed in eagerly.

Then Mrs. Mulcahey turned toward my sister.

"He likes to climb trees and he had an accident and he fell," Susan agreed.

That was what our father had told us to say.

He fell out of a tree. We were all falling out of trees all the time.

I almost said something, but I bit my tongue. I knew if I told the truth, I'd be killed. My father hated having anything to do with teachers, cops, doctors—you name it. He'd murder me for sure if I told.

The principal and the nurse all seemed satisfied with the explanation that Joseph had fallen out of a tree and the three of us were sent back to our classes. They'd done their job. They'd gone through the motions. They'd asked the questions they were supposed to ask. But obviously they didn't really care about helping us.

Abandonment and neglect were clear and easy to define, and the police could do something about it. "Disciplining" children, though, was something different—at least it was back then. Basically, the feeling was that you didn't tell parents how to raise their kids; you didn't stick your nose in other people's business. Besides, the schoolteachers looked on us as bad kids; they figured kids as tough to handle as we were would need a lot of disciplining.

But what it came down to was that we were an embarrassment. We were the school's dirty little secret.

One day while I was in the woods I spotted a tomcat on the prowl. He stopped for a moment, and then he sprang. I saw a blur of motion. Then I saw that the tomcat had gotten a hold of a little chipmunk. The chipmunk had no chance. I stood there and watched the cat beat that little chipmunk up and put the chipmunk's head in his mouth. All that cat had to do was just twitch his jaw and he could take the chipmunk's head right off completely. But he didn't kill him immediately. Whenever the cat came close to killing the chipmunk, he'd stop to play with it. Then the chipmunk would flop down and just lie there, playing possum. But the tomcat knew better than to believe the chipmunk was dead, and he'd whack him with one paw and whack him with the other paw, and then grab him by the leg with his teeth. But the chipmunk still played possum, probably hoping that if it pretended to be dead long enough, the tom would just go away. Then all of a sudden the chipmunk tried to escape. And *boom!*—the cat was right on top of it. The chipmunk was no match. He was absolutely no match.

During the whole thing I knew the chipmunk was aware I was watching. But I couldn't kick the cat and yell, "Get away from that chipmunk!" I was almost in a trance. I just stood there a few feet from the chipmunk and let the cat do what he wanted. But I knew what the chipmunk was going through. I knew how much he wanted to run, and that he couldn't get away. What that chipmunk was feeling, *I* was feeling. The same helplessness. Such a strong cat and such a helpless little chipmunk. I stood there and watched without doing a thing, not because I took pleasure from seeing the chipmunk get killed, but because I was almost paralyzed. It was such a familiar feeling to me. That was me I was seeing in that chipmunk. That was me the cat was sinking its teeth into. That was me being torn to pieces.

Sixth grade is a tough time no matter where you go to school. When I was in sixth grade, the popular boys my age all pretended they were in a gang, like they were wise guys. I didn't fit into their crowd. Among them I had one major enemy, and that was Roger.

Roger wore glasses, and he was a skinny kid. We were both in the same grade, but he was a little bit bigger than I was. Roger made me his enemy the first time he laid eyes on me. He called me nasty names, and eventually he got rough. Every chance he had—especially during recess—he'd whack me on the head and pull my hair and push me around so I landed—facedown—on the pavement.

Roger liked to do this sort of thing most when girls were around. It was his way of showing off for them. He never really hurt me—but that wasn't the point. Being humiliated is a lot worse than getting a scraped knee. Roger's harassment developed into a routine. It went on every day, sometimes twice a day, at lunch and at recess. The only time I had a break was after school when he had to take a bus home. It always came as a great relief when he was out sick. Unfortunately, this happened all too rarely.

I'd always considered school a refuge from the horrors at home, but now going to school became horrible, too. Not that what Roger was doing to me was anything like what my father did to me, but the feeling of being terrorized for no good reason was much the same. Finally, I couldn't take it anymore. *I can do something about this kid.* I couldn't do anything about my father, but I could do something about Roger.

I knew I'd have to confront him sooner or later and that we'd end up coming to blows. A show of force was the only thing that was going to work with Roger. The only trouble was, I'd never been in a fight before. This would be my first time, and I was afraid. I was completely inexperienced with this sort of thing. What would I do when we came face to face? Where would I hit him? I started thinking about it. What's the worst he could do to me? He could beat me up, he could hurt me, but nothing he could do to me would even come close to the beatings I got from my father. This kid couldn't punch me half as hard as I'd already been punched. So I figured, even if worse came to worst, I could deal with it. I knew how to block myself. I knew how to tighten my skin. I knew how to hit. Roger could pull my hair all he wanted. What did I have to lose? The only real danger was if we were caught and the school sent a note home.

Even though I was mentally ready to take Roger on, I still needed to have some idea about how to fight—what moves to make, what parts of the body to target. Then I realized that I'd already gotten some lessons in fistfighting. I remembered Westerns we used to watch on TV. John Wayne or Gary Cooper would saunter into a saloon and suddenly a fight would break out. The hero would beat up a half-dozen bad guys without getting a scratch himself. He'd punch a guy in the face, and the guy would go down. And then John Wayne would pick him up by his shirt collar and whack him again. If this was how it was done on TV, I thought, then this must be the way things happened in real life. That's how you fight, I figured, that's how you beat somebody up. Having John Wayne and Gary Cooper as my teachers reassured me that I'd know what to do when the time came. And with the beatings I got every day, I realized that my father had given me a few lessons in fighting, too.

I bided my time, putting up with Roger's insults and shoving, waiting for the perfect opportunity. Then one afternoon, at recess, I spotted Roger across the playground. There were no teachers anywhere to be seen. This was the moment. Look at this little twig, I said to myself, you can take him. I was trying to give myself courage. He was coming toward me, and he had a friend with him, but the friend had never done anything to me. He was happy to remain on the sidelines, cheering Roger on.

Roger didn't expect what was coming. I turned around and I whacked him—clobbered him in the face so hard that his glasses flew into the air and he went down. I guess I had a good right hook. I clocked him. That punch really made him pay attention.

"Get up quick, Roger, before the teacher sees," his friend hissed. It was like his friend was taking my side. He probably thought he'd be in trouble, too, if we were caught.

Roger was still on the ground, crying. In a daze, he finally picked himself up and retrieved his glasses. He was relieved to find they weren't broken.

I was surprised at how easy things had gone. I'd expected a bloody, knockdown battle and here it was over in less than thirty seconds.

There was a possibility Roger could go to a teacher and tell on me, but if he did that, he was going to get in trouble, too. So I felt a pretty overwhelming surge of power. I gave him a warning.

"If you tell on me," I said, "I'm going to beat the piss out of you." He sniffled and brushed away his tears. He seemed to hesitate for a moment. Then he said, "Okay, I won't pick on you anymore." I guess it was his way of saying he was sorry.

No teacher ever found out what had happened. And after that no one bothered me. The word had gotten out. The kids thought I was a tough guy. I didn't have to take this sort of abuse from Roger or anybody else. It was amazing that I was able to change the whole situation just like that. One punch changed everything.

could have been a straight-A student. In spite of all the chaos at home and the long stretches of time I was kept out of school, I still got good grades. I was a smart, sharp kid, and did well right through the fifth grade.

In sixth grade, though, this all changed. The problems at home didn't increase or decrease, but they were different. For one thing, Ma was leaving more and more often. After my father had brought her back from Haverhill, we'd thought that that would be the end of it, that she wouldn't run again. But we were wrong. She was a runner. That was her nature. She'd run to her parents, she'd run to her sister, and once in a while she'd take refuge at the home of a friend named Rita.

Whether she took us with her or not depended on the circumstances. Before the state agencies almost took us away, she ran away alone. Afterward she would take us because she didn't want to be nailed by the courts for neglecting and abandoning her children again. After a while, though, she wore out her welcome and had nowhere left to go. Sometimes she was so desperate she'd run anyway and find shelter in a church. So we'd end up spending the night sleeping in the pews. She did this for years. She ran and ran and ran.

Ma's frequent flights began to take a toll on my schooling. I'd miss weeks and months at a time. Some years I missed anywhere from forty-five to sixty days of school. Often the school had no idea where I was. When I reached sixth grade, I really started to go downhill. It got so bad I didn't have any idea which grade I belonged in, because I'd been ripped out of school so often I never finished a full term. How I ended up beginning seventh grade was a real mystery, because I wasn't really sure I passed the sixth. Apparently I did. I was so confused I was ready to start sixth grade all over again. I just didn't know.

Many years later, when I got hold of my school records, I saw the notation "whereabouts unknown" next to my name on an absentee report. For some reason the school authorities never tried to keep track of us. You'd have thought someone would have reported our absence to truant officers, but if this happened I never knew about it. What my mother did, pulling us out of school for so long at a time, was probably illegal. But to my knowledge no one ever came to our door or phoned to demand an explanation. Maybe they were afraid of finding out what was really going on in the Theodore household, because then they'd have to take action. That might be why, even after the principal saw with her own eyes the kind of abuse we were subjected to, she didn't do anything. In my mind they're as guilty as my parents; they were accomplices, because they stood by and pretended nothing was happening.

For seventh grade I had to go to a different school in Methuen, and because it was farther away, I had to take a bus. The new school was an ugly brick building, gray on the bottom and a sort of tan on top. It looked like a high-security prison. The bus ride took us across the bridge over the Merrimack River—the same bridge I'd marveled at as a little kid, sitting up on the hill at night. By now, I was beginning to get a pretty good idea of the local geography. I had more of a sense of where the highway led. Little by little the outside world was opening up.

Seventh grade changed everything for me. I'd been a pretty good kid up until then, but now I was becoming known as something of a troublemaker. I was fourteen years old and constantly getting into fights with other kids. Once I'd beaten up Roger, I knew I could take on anyone. If somebody looked at me funny I was ready to clock him. My grades sank accordingly: I was getting D's and F's. But I didn't care anymore.

I was expelled three weeks before the end of the school year. My father didn't mind. Actually, he was happy about it. He wanted me to fail.

In spite of my expulsion, I went back to school the next term. I was really amazed that I was starting the eighth grade, since I couldn't figure out why they'd let me pass the seventh. In any case, I knew I was getting to an age when my father was going to make me quit school for good so he could put me to work. I knew this would probably be my last chance to make something of my education. I decided to put in a real effort this time. And it paid off: I went from a D and F student to a B student. Remarkably, I even got a couple of A's—pretty good considering I'd done nothing for three years. Doing well in school was a way for me to fight back. I knew my father wanted me to fail—he always told me how stupid I was—so I was determined to do well.

Good grades or bad grades, it made no difference to my father. He thought school was a waste of time.

"As soon as you're old enough you're quitting school and going to work," my father would say to us. That was what we had to look forward to. When my father got wind of a law that permitted a parent to sign a kid out of school at the age of fourteen to get a job, he went wild. It was as if the law had been written especially for his benefit. Back in the late sixties and early seventies, it wasn't as difficult as it is now to get working papers at a younger age.

If I had been honest with myself, I'd have realized that I actually did like school, deep down. But I told myself I hated school. And I hated it because my father had taught me to hate it. He started drumming it into our heads early on: *You don't need to go to school.* We all believed him— every single one of us—all my brothers and sisters. There wasn't one kid in my family who liked school. *Those stupid teachers. They don't know nothing. You don't need that. You got to go to work. Go to work, bring money in.* Or he'd tell us, "Look at me—I can't write. Why do you need to?" (In fact, he could write, and he was pretty good at arithmetic, too.)

But that wasn't the only reason he didn't want me to get an education. He hadn't gotten much of one himself, and he was in trouble a lot at school, so he probably felt something was lacking inside. What made him most afraid was that, if he allowed me to continue in school, I might end up becoming smarter than he was. And he couldn't let that happen. No one was ever allowed to be smarter than him.

More documents related to the court case against my parents turned up as I dug. There were petitions like this one for all six of us:

NOTICE TO
THE DEPARTMENT OF PUBLIC WELFARE,
STATE HOUSE, BOSTON, MASS.

You are hereby notified that a Petition has heretofore been filed with the District Court of Lawrence by the Department of Public Welfare, alleging on behalf of Wayne Brian Theodore, a child under sixteen years, presently of 46 Bridge Street in Methuen in said County of Essex, that said child is without necessary and proper physical care or is growing up under conditions or circumstances damaging to said child's sound character development, or lacks proper attention of (his) parent(s) and whose said parent(s)— lawful Guardian—are unwilling, incompetent or unavailable to provide such care and praying that this Court issue a precept to bring said child before said Court and summons the said parent(s)—to appear before said Court and show cause why said child should not be committed to the custody of the Department of Public Welfare of said Commonwealth, or make such other order regarding the care and custody of said child as said Court shall deem appropriate. . . .

Then I came to a description of our condition when we were taken into custody by the state:

"When first seen on August 22nd . . . Wayne and his siblings were all thin, scantily clad in dirty clothes, barefooted, and stringy haired, grimy, and frightened. . . ." In the MSPCC report the "baby"—that would be my brother Christopher—was described as having "blistered areas on the back of his head and heels, apparently from rubbing himself as he lay unattended. There were also unidentifiable welts and abrasions on his head, and a very severe rash in his genital area."

He would have been three months old at the time. How could anybody leave a baby alone like that?

There was something else about me in the report:

> "It was observed that Wayne was nearly incapable of forming a relationship with anyone, and that he had many fears, including fear of the loss of mother, and of being cut by his father while having his hair cut. He was abusive of other children and destroyed his toys. Both Wayne and the baby had severe urine burns in their genital area. Wayne seemed to have an organic intestinal illness, marked by very frequent, loose soiling.

The report said we'd been placed in the Tewkesbury Hospital when I was three years old. Together with my two older brothers and my sister Susan, we had been left to fend for ourselves in a house full of rats, garbage, urine, and rotten feces.

I began to realize that when you have certain information that's suppressed in your memory, even though you don't remember it, it still makes a difference in your life. It did in Brian's, and it did in mine. Those memories fester and begin to poison you without your being aware of it. You don't know why you're so messed up because your mind has blocked it out. It's like a high-tech computer system designed to protect you.

But no computer system is perfect. Sometimes it freezes—it crashes. And that was what was about to happen to me.

never finished eighth grade. It didn't matter that I'd worked hard to get good grades. From my father's standpoint, I was ready to go to work and bring in some extra money for my family, extra money for him. I had no trouble getting a job right off the bat. Because I looked a good deal older than my age, I simply walked into a local McDonald's and told the manager that I was seventeen and needed a job. I'd chosen to try McDonald's, first because it was within easy walking distance of my house. It was located on Pleasant Valley Street, not far from my old elementary school.

I was hired as a janitor, to start. That job immediately brought about some welcome changes in my life. For one thing, I had better—and cleaner—clothes, because I had to wear a uniform. It meant that I was allowed to wash the uniform in the tub every evening. And now I didn't have to share my clothes with my brothers. No one was allowed to mess with your clothes if you were working. That was a rule enforced by my father.

There was another benefit to being employed: I started eating better. Not only did I have bologna—that was quite a treat for me—but now I had a daily supply of burgers and fries. I didn't take these privileges for granted; I worked really hard and did whatever I had to do to make sure I kept the job. I had another incentive, too—the threat of getting another beating if I lost the job for any reason.

I didn't have anything to worry about, though. It wasn't long before I was promoted from janitor to working on the floor. I'd come in at five-thirty in the morning to set up. I was the designated "set-up man."

That meant washing the floors and getting the kitchen ready, turning on the grills for the burgers and turning on the deep-fryers to heat up the French fries. The manager saw that I was a conscientious worker. And he realized that I had a brain, as well. I really enjoyed the attention he was giving me. For the first time in my life I was being acknowledged for doing something positive, and it motivated me to work even harder. I was far and away the best worker, and I was putting in so many hours— forty-five a week—that my weekly paycheck was usually about ninety dollars, pretty good money for a fourteen-year-old. I probably would have been made manager eventually, if I'd stayed.

But my father interfered. There were two things my father didn't like about my job at McDonald's. One was that I was out of work early in the afternoon after finishing my shift and had time to kill before he came home from work. That gave me several hours of freedom when there was no one to supervise me or keep track of what I was doing. His second complaint was that it wasn't paying me well enough. He was convinced I could make more money (for him) elsewhere.

So I ended up working at a grocery store in Methuen called Keeley Farms. The job paid a little more, but it was farther away. So instead of being able to go home, I'd have to wait for my father to pick me up after work. Often, this meant waiting for hours.

Because my father was never one to be inconvenienced for the sake of his kids, he forced me to quit that job, too, and find a job closer to his job in Merrimac. I found work at a mill run by a company called Oomphies. Now I was making close to double the money I'd earned at McDonald's—about $180 every week.

Soon after taking the job at Oomphies, I persuaded the manager to hire my brother John. Then Michael went to work for a factory across the street. When we'd finish our shifts in the late afternoon, the three of us would meet and wait for my father to pick us up. He'd get out at the same time, but that didn't mean we could count on him to turn up right then. Some nights we'd stand at the corner in front of the factory until ten o'clock waiting for him. It was no secret why he was late. We knew he was getting drunk at some local dive. A couple of nights he didn't show up at all, but we couldn't leave the corner, because if we weren't there when he finally got around to collecting us, there'd be hell to pay.

Most of my sisters ended up going to work for my father, too—even Gail, who was the eighth child. When she got a job at a nursing home, she begged my father to let her live with Susan, who had a boyfriend by this time and was living in an apartment in Methuen. He reluctantly agreed, but on one condition—that she continued to give him at least half her paycheck. Otherwise she'd have had to stay home and work and give him her *whole* paycheck. It was extortion, pure and simple.

Eventually there were five of us with jobs, and my father took all the money—five hundred to six hundred dollars a week from us, plus the money he made from his own job. He had a nice little racket going. He wasn't one to show a lot of excitement on his face, but he was obviously getting what he wanted out of this arrangement.

Once we started working, my father eased up a little on the beatings. But the abuse didn't end completely. For example, missing a day of work guaranteed a beating. It didn't matter if you were running a fever of 102—he'd still work himself into a frenzy. A sick day meant a day's less salary.

"And if you ever get fired, you're dead," he warned.

I hated my job at Oomphies. It was an old, dark factory—a dungeon, just like home, with wire on the dirty windows and no sunlight coming in. It felt like a prison to me. I was working up the courage to quit in spite of, or maybe because of, my father's threats. I knew this would be a turning point for me. I was fifteen years old and becoming stronger every day, and I was beginning to doubt my father's physical strength. The older I got, the harder he beat me, but the harder he beat me, the stronger I became. Was he getting weaker, or was I getting stronger? I had to test his strength, his power, and I had to do it out in the open, rather than just fighting him in my mind, secretly, like my trips into the woods.

I finally found the courage to quit my job at Oomphies. I knew what I was letting myself in for. To postpone the inevitable beating, I made up a story so my father wouldn't know what had really happened. I knew it wouldn't be long before he found out the truth—he always did—but for some reason I didn't feel any sense of urgency to find another job. So the next day, instead of running right out and searching for work, I just hung around the house. Finally, I thought, I should make some effort to get a job, and I began browsing through the Yellow Pages. I was going to write down a few numbers, but I didn't have a pen.

I opened the top drawer of an end table where my father put all sorts of stuff. Going through a drawer was forbidden, but since no one was in the house at the time—my mother and Gail were in the backyard—I didn't think anything of it.

How could I have known that my freedom was waiting for me in that desk drawer? All I had to do was grab it.

When I peered inside the drawer, the first thing I saw was a form with my name on it. It was from the IRS. I didn't know very much about income tax stuff. I knew there was something called a W-2 form, but back then I didn't have any concept of what that meant. How could I? I'd never seen any W-2s, with all the jobs I'd held. That was true for all my brothers and sisters. We were never allowed to touch the mail. My father got all of my W-2s.

I didn't understand that employers automatically deducted taxes from your paycheck and that at the end of the year it might turn out that the government owed you back some of the money. It was just something that hadn't ever occurred to me. So my father kept us ignorant, and then cheated us blind.

He had gone to H&R Block and asked one of their accountants to do my tax return. And then my father had signed my name to it. When the refund came a month or so later, he'd endorsed the check and cashed it. From what I could tell, he'd been doing this for a couple of years. The proof was right there in the drawer. Only a few months before, he'd cashed a refund check of mine in the amount of three hundred dollars. *Three hundred dollars!* And I wasn't the only one, either. He was pulling the same trick with every one of us who were due refunds.

The more I thought about what he'd done, the angrier I became. I felt like such a dope. Here was my father exploiting his kids, pulling in as much as five-hundred dollars a week from us, and then he turned around and stole our refund checks right from under our noses. *What else is there in this drawer?* I wondered. There was no telling what other damning evidence I might find if I looked. I dug further. Although I didn't come across any more tax forms, I did discover something even better—a set of car keys.

They were lying at the bottom of the drawer, under the papers. I recognized them right away. They were the keys to the car my father had just bought. He kept it parked at the bottom of the hill. This was his extra car. It was only three years old, with less than 100,000 miles on it. It was a real fancy car, too, that we'd bought for him without our knowing it—a 1971 Mach I Mustang, a whooped-up hot rod, a real "muscle car."

I stared at the keys. They glinted in the lamplight, beckoning me to grab them. I was excited—but I was scared, too. I knew what would happen if I gave in to the temptation.

The house was very still. I could hear my mother talking to Gail outside. This was my opportunity. He'd stolen from me; he was stealing from all of us. Worse, he'd committed these thefts without us ever being aware of it. He liked to think he was pulling all the strings.

I thought about all this, and it made me furious. I reached down and took the keys. Then I put all the papers back so he'd never be able to tell that anything had been touched.

I walked out of the house and started down the road toward the car. I was all pumped up, but I was very nervous. At first I wasn't planning on taking the car; that wasn't in my mind. I just wanted to sit in it and maybe listen to the radio. Just knowing that I'd invaded his territory and sat behind the wheel in his hot rod would give me a certain satisfaction.

He'd draped a plastic sheet over the car to protect it from the weather. He treated his new car better than he did his kids. I slipped the cover off the car, rolled it up, and put it behind a tree. I kept glancing back up toward my house. I was way down at the end of the road, but I knew I was still in danger of being spotted from the yard. If Gail or my mother had turned and looked they could have seen me. Luckily, they never did. I was amazed I was actually doing this and getting away with it. I opened the car door and climbed inside. It felt so powerful to sit behind the wheel. I was beginning to get a little confidence now. I put the key in the ignition, but I still didn't turn it on.

Then I thought back to the tax forms. I was seething. How could he do that to us? How could a father deliberately rob his own children? And he probably figured we'd never catch him.

He was wrong.

How could I get back at him? The answer was right in my hands. All I had to do was turn the key. I could take his damn car! A few minutes before, the idea of taking his car had been unimaginable, but now it seemed like the best thing—the only thing—to do. The only way to show my father that he couldn't get away with this kind of garbage. There was only one problem: I was only fifteen, and I didn't know how to drive.

All the same, I figured I could get it moving. The car was an automatic—that much I knew. I put it into neutral. Well, okay, I thought, now what? Given that the remaining stretch went downhill all I had to do was give the car a rolling start and I'd reach the road without any trouble. How I'd get it back up the driveway was another story. I didn't want to think about that now. So I got out and pushed the car and got it rolling. Then I jumped back in and steered it toward the road. This was tricky, because I still had the gates to contend with. It was only after I'd opened and shut them and gotten the car on the main road that I felt comfortable about turning on the ignition. The engine surged in response—a wonderful sound mixed with a huge rush of something I wasn't used to feeling. Later, I figured out what that something was—it was power.

For the first five seconds, I had the same thought over and over: *I'm driving his car, I'm driving his goddamn car.* There was nothing like it. It was like going into the woods, but with more possibilities. I laughed, and my laughter seemed really loud, even over the engine's roar. At first, they were nervous laughs, that made me sound like I was hiccuping. But after a while, I was really and truly laughing.

I wasn't sure whether my mother or Gail would notice that the car was missing. I knew that if they did, there was no turning back. I couldn't trust my mother to keep a secret from my father.

So, why not? I thought. *What have I got to lose? I might as well go for a ride.* I put my foot to the gas. The rubber tires smoked and suddenly, I was barreling down the highway toward the center of Methuen, learning how to drive as I went.

I was so exhilarated that I just kept going faster and faster. Then I glanced at the speedometer. To my great amazement, I'd run the Mach up to 120 miles an hour. Even I knew how fast that was. I was doing 120 mph, zipping along on the freeway. Why stop? So I just kept going. I shot right through Methuen and went all the way to Andover, and then on to North Andover. Suddenly it dawned on me that I was driving in the area near where my father worked. If he spotted the car, I'd be busted. It wasn't the cops I was afraid of, even though I was way over the speed limit and driving without a license! I was just imagining my father stepping outside the factory and standing there, maybe talking to one of his buddies, and then glancing up and seeing me. *Hey, that's funny, that looks like the car I just bought. Hey, wait a minute, that is the car I just bought! And who's that jerk behind the wheel? Is that who I think it is?*

Suddenly reality set in. I had to put an end to my little joy ride and get back home before my father did. And I just had to hope no one had realized that the car was gone to begin with. It was about three in the afternoon, so I figured I still had enough time. And now that I'd gotten the hang of driving, I no longer had to worry about how to get the car back up the driveway.

When I reached the driveway, I stopped and checked to see if anyone was around. When I was sure I was safe, I drove up, passing successfully through the first gate. But as I approached the second gate, I shut the engine off. Even though I was on a small incline, I was going fast enough to roll it back into its parking space. Then I covered it over with the sheet of plastic and even took the precaution of sweeping the ground around it so my father wouldn't see the tire tracks.

My mother and sister were still busy in the backyard. Astonishingly, they hadn't seen me pull it in. I couldn't get over how lucky I'd been.

As I walked back up the hill, Michael stepped out of the house. As soon as I looked at him I could tell he'd seen me put the car back.

Sure enough, he said he'd seen everything. "I'm going to tell Ma what you did," he said.

I was thrown into a panic. "Please, Michael, don't say anything. You know what he'll do to me if he finds out."

Michael was adamant. No, he said, he'd have to tell our father. That was all there was to it.

"What have I done to you? Why are you doing this?" I begged him not to rat on me. I pleaded with him. I was almost in tears.

He wasn't angry at me. He had no reason to rat on me, but I think he was afraid that if he didn't say anything the consequences would be worse for him. And he might have been a little envious that I'd dared to do something he'd never do. He just walked back into the house. I quickly put the keys back in the drawer where I'd gotten them, and hoped that Michael would change his mind.

How could this happen? I'd almost gotten away with it. I'd thought of everything; my father never would have known. And now my own brother—the brother who was closest to me—was going to rat on me! It was unbelievable.

Worse, by this time we'd gotten a phone, so news could travel fast. My father would know in an instant what I'd done. It was as if my father was telepathic, because even before Michael could say anything the phone rang and my mother went to answer it.

I knew it had to be my father. As my mother was talking to him, asking when he expected to be home for supper, Michael just sidled over to her and said, "Ma."

"What is it? Can't you see I'm talking to your father?"

I was standing a few feet away, signaling desperately to Michael—*no, no, no, don't do it!* But he refused even to glance in my direction.

"Ma," he said again, "there's something I got to tell you."

"What is it, Michael?"

Then he told her. The blood drained from her face. This was serious business. She looked over at me in disbelief. I could hear my father's voice through the phone. "Ruth, Ruth, what's going on there?"

My blood was rising in a combination of dread and fury. I didn't want to listen anymore. I turned and walked out of the house.

A few minutes later Michael came outside to announce that my mother had told my father what I'd done, and now he was on a rampage. He was leaving work right away, Michael said, and he was coming home to deal with me. Michael may have been a tattletale because he didn't want a beating, but there was no question that he was getting a kick out of my situation.

I knew what would happen when my father got home. I figured if I was going to get the kind of beating he planned for me, then he'd surely kill me. I was already in trouble for quitting the job at Oomphies.

Stealing pocket change, even fifty bucks, was one thing. So was wetting the bed. But in the crazy universe of the Theodore family—unpredictable as things were—I knew this much: Taking the car meant death.

I wasn't going to give him the chance. I did the only thing that made sense: I ran away.

I was free for the first time in my life. I was fifteen years old and about to plunge into a world I knew nothing about, but I felt incredibly relieved. I was so excited to find myself on my own that I couldn't think of the future. I wasn't scared, because the idea of being free was so new to me. It would take time to get used to, but I still had to figure out my next move: Where was I going to go?

By this time my grandparents were long dead. I hadn't really made any friends at work, either. I considered going to my big sister Susan's apartment, but that would be the first place my father would look for me. It would have been nice to step up to a door, ring a bell, and have somebody open up and say, "Hey, Wayne, come in, it's great to see you." Well, that wasn't going to happen. There weren't any welcome mats being put out for me.

All that mattered was that I make myself as scarce as I could. I didn't want my father to find me, so I kept off the main highway. I have no idea how many miles I covered. I probably didn't get very far. On the other hand, having never run off like this before, I could have been halfway to the moon. I had no money. I was lost.

More important, though, I was happy, and I was free. No matter where I ended up, I figured it was bound to be better than the place I'd come from. The feeling was exhilarating, and I wanted to revel in it for as long as I could.

As I thought back over the afternoon, I couldn't believe how much I'd done. If I'd never opened that drawer and found that tax information, I never would have ended up taking the car or running away. It was astonishing to me how, because of one small thing, you can turn your whole life around. It was almost as if those keys weren't the keys to the car as much as the keys to my freedom.

I didn't have to worry about getting a beating for getting home late. I wasn't going home. Not ever. I was still afraid, though—not of what was ahead of me, but of what might be gaining on me from behind. Each time a car passed and its headlights streaked across my face, I had the creepy sensation it might be him. I stayed close to the shadows. I tried to suppress the fear. *Listen, Wayne,* I told myself, *relax. He won't be able to find you. It's a big world.*

Because it was early summer, the night was warm. It would be no big deal to sleep outside. After a while I came to a residential neighborhood where I found a park.

I bummed a cigarette from a kid who was hanging around the entrance and went inside to have a smoke. I had no idea just how exhausted I was until I dropped down on a bench. I'd no sooner gotten the cigarette lit and had a few puffs than I dozed off. When I woke several hours later I saw an ugly red burn on my palm. I'd been so exhausted that I'd never felt a thing.

If I was going to make it on my own I had to find food and shelter. I'd survived all those beatings and the abuse at home and I knew how to forage for food in the woods, so how hard could it be?

The neighborhood was more familiar now that it was daylight. After walking for about half an hour I came to a bunch of kids hanging out in a parking lot. I spotted a kid I knew from school whose name was Tom. I didn't know him well, but he nodded in recognition—that was all the encouragement I needed. At first I just stood around, listening to what they were saying. When one kid told a joke I joined in the laughter, even though I had no idea what was so funny. I was just trying to make myself fit in. I watched their faces and took my cue from their expressions as to how I should act.

"Hey, let's go to my house and grab some food," Tom said.

The other kids followed him, and I tagged along.

Tom and his mother lived in an apartment in a complex nearby.

When I saw all the food Tom put out, I could barely contain myself. Sandwiches, apples, cookies, potato chips—all free for the taking. When

I reached for a cheese sandwich no one stopped me. It was amazing. I began to wolf it down.

The other kids were staring at me. "Hey, Theodore, nobody's going to take it away from you," Tom said.

I stopped gobbling for a second, and thought fast. "That's what my old man says."

Everyone got a kick out of that. They all laughed. That was a relief. No one suspected a thing.

When Tom's mom came home a little later he didn't rush to turn the TV off, which was what I'd have done if I'd been in my house. His mother smelled like flowers. As soon as she walked in I felt safe. My father wasn't about to come barging into somebody else's house.

"We're going to Aunt Martha's tonight," his mother said.

Tom made a face. Then he shrugged. "See you guys tomorrow," he said.

So the rest of us piled out of the house. Now what was I going to do?

"Let's go to the pool," said a kid named Kevin.

I followed the group to the pool and dropped down into a lounge chair.

"Come on in," Kevin urged me.

"But I don't have a suit."

Kevin shrugged and dived in, joining the others. So I spent the rest of the day watching them swim. When it got dark, they all went home. Because I didn't have a home, I walked vaguely toward the parking lot. I didn't know where else to go. I found a bench and lay down on it. I was hungry and tired, but what worried me most was the possibility my father would find me. Or maybe the police would grab me.

But nothing happened. Nobody came for me at all, and it was very quiet. I liked it that way. If I'd been at home I'd have been crushed next to my brother on the bunk bed, listening to my parents have another of their fights. This was much better.

This was the first day of my life that I didn't fear a beating—my first real full day of freedom.

The next morning I felt a hand clamped on my shoulder. I jerked awake, my hand balled defensively into a fist.

But it was only Tom. He was surprised to see me there. "You going back home?"

I shook my head. "I can't take my old man anymore."

I didn't need to say more. Tom seemed to know what I meant. "You can sleep in my mom's car as long as she doesn't find out."

We went over to the lot and he opened the back door of an old black Buick Electra.

The back seat of an old Buick is a huge improvement over a park bench.

Then Tom went into the house and came out wearing bathing trunks, with another pair in his hand. "Want to come for a swim?"

I grinned, amazed at my luck.

"Sure, that'd be great."

I hung in tight with these guys. They became my world. I paid careful attention, and I was a quick study. I learned to talk the way they talked, saying "Hey, man" instead of "Hello," and "See you around" instead of "Good-bye." When they ate, I ate, too, and eventually I slowed down and learned to chew. When they smoked grass, I'd get some hits, too, and then we'd all mellow out and eat some more. By now they all knew I didn't want to go home, and occasionally one of the guys would invite me to spend the night at his place, so I could have a sofa or a floor to sleep on instead of the Buick.

I became one of the gang. I didn't have a shower to use, but I could go swimming every day, which meant I probably smelled way better than I had when I lived with my mother and father.

So that was my first summer away from home.

I was still on the run, though. There was always the possibility that my father would find me. For one thing, where I was staying was just on the other side of town from where my family lived—a twenty-minute drive. It wasn't as if I was hiding out so much as I was on my guard, constantly looking over my shoulder, knowing he might show up someday and snatch me back into the hell I'd finally succeeded in escaping.

Then one day I noticed that Tom seemed on edge. I asked him what was the matter. "Last night my mom wanted to know if I was letting one of my pals sleep in the car," he said. "I told her no. She'd kill me if she saw you there."

I wasn't too upset. I knew I wouldn't be able to use the car indefinitely, but I asked if I could spend just one more night in the car and then in the morning I'd make other arrangements.

He shook his head. He didn't want to risk it.

Then I said, "Hey, I've got an idea."

When I told him what I was thinking he looked at me like I was crazy. "You'd do that?"

"Sure I would."

And that's how I ended up locked in the trunk for eight hours.

The whole time I was at Tom's, I was meeting new people every day. Without even thinking about it, I went from being too shy to say anything more than "Hi," to making new friends. One was a girl about my age named Judy who took a liking to me. When she heard that I could no longer use the Buick she told me that her mother was away for a few weeks, so I could sleep on their living room sofa. And I'd have the luxury of using a real shower, and—because they had a washer and dryer—clean clothes.

That summer turned out to be a pretty happy time. I was learning how to become independent. I was growing stronger. Yet I wouldn't know how strong I really was until I came face to face with my father.

Sometimes I'd feel a sudden pang and miss my mother and brothers and sisters. I called them a couple of times to find out how they were doing, and whether they missed *me*. But I didn't reveal where I was. As difficult as things got for me, figuring out where I'd be from one day to the next, I was too happy being free to ever want to go back.

But after two weeks, I had to leave Judy's. I asked around, and no one else had anywhere I could crash. So I asked Susan if I could stay at her apartment. She said yes, but we both knew I was taking a big risk. My mother had run away again, and my father was out looking for her. I guess I should have been prepared when he stopped by Susan's to see if Ma had taken refuge with her. He didn't find Ma, but he did find me.

He didn't seem surprised to see me. I had a feeling that one of the siblings I was in touch with had tipped him off.

After months of imagining what would happen when I finally faced my father, when it actually happened I was just stunned by the reality of it. I was staring right at him, but I couldn't quite grasp the fact that he was there.

He said hello, politely. Then he did something I wasn't used to seeing. He smiled.

A moment later Christopher, now ten, trailed in behind him. I learned later that my father had planned all this. Maybe he'd brought Christopher along to reassure me.

Once he'd looked around to make sure Ma wasn't there, he beckoned me outside. "Come on, Wayne, there's nothing to be afraid of."

Various scenarios ran through my mind. Should I go with him? Should I refuse?

I decided to go. After all, I couldn't run forever. Sooner or later, I'd have to confront him. Better now—when I was alert—than later, when he might catch me unexpectedly.

Still, when I walked out the door I was feeling nervous. I couldn't let him see it, though. *I'm strong now, I can take him.* I had to believe that. I had to have faith.

As soon as I stepped outside Susan's building, I saw Christopher take a few steps back. It was as if he knew that something was about to happen and that it wouldn't be pretty. I looked around for my father. Out of the corner of my eye I caught a blur of motion. Before I could react he grabbed me by the hair and hurled me to the ground. When I looked up his fist was in my face. *Now I'm in for it. Here comes the beating.*

"Don't you ever say anything about our family or anything that we do," he yelled. "You say a word and you're dead meat, you hear?"

What was so weird was that his fist was still hanging in the air. This was totally unexpected. By now my nose should have been a bloody pulp. *Why doesn't he hit me?* I wondered. *What's wrong with this picture?*

Then something occurred to me. At first I thought it was impossible, but the longer that fist stayed in the air the more the realization sank in. *He isn't hitting me because he's scared.*

He was growing red in the face from shouting at me, but I couldn't have cared less. He could threaten and bully me all he wanted, but I still had the power. It was a power I hadn't had before—the power of being out in the world, in contact with other people. *I might tell.* Telling was a very, very big thing. And it was a shameful thing, too—to tell the people on the outside what was really going on. That was what my father feared most, and as long as I had that power I was safe. Or so I thought.

My father didn't force me to go home, but I knew it was a risk to stay at Susan's. He might change his mind and come back. For weeks I drifted from place to place. I was living like a bum, sleeping in one place for a night or two, and then moving on. My life in Methuen was starting to fall apart. I realized that I'd better get my act together.

I hooked up with a kid named Ted who lived in Lawrence, eight miles away. He said he knew a guy who'd give us a job painting. If the job came through, Ted said, we could find a place to live and split the rent.

The next day we met the contractor Ted knew, Mr. Davis. He told me to put on a pair of crisp white overalls, and then he drove me over to a large house that must have belonged to a millionaire.

"Do you know how to paint?" he asked.

"Sure," I said. I wasn't telling the truth. I hadn't done any house painting before, but I figured, how hard could it be?

"Good, let me see."

I lifted off the lid of the paint can, spattering myself in the process. I hoped Mr. Davis wouldn't hit me too hard once he realized I had no idea what I was doing.

He watched me for a minute, and then handed me a wooden stirrer. "Stir it first," he said kindly.

As I stirred, more paint splashed over the side of the can.

"You're wasting paint." Then he took the brush and demonstrated. "Like this—hold the brush between your thumb and index finger."

I tried to follow his example under his watchful gaze.

"Better," he said. "Move your wrist with the brush."

I was beginning to get the hang of it. Mr. Davis nodded. I had no experience, but I got the job anyway. I was thrilled.

I went to work immediately. As days passed, and then weeks, I got better at it. I was finally learning a skill—not like putting shoes on an assembly line or packing them in a shipping container, but something that would allow me to improve my living situation, give me a better home. And I had more incentive: I started to crave Mr. Davis's approval. This man who didn't even know me had put his faith in me. I was so grateful that I wanted to show him he was right to trust me.

A few weeks later Ted and I rented an apartment over a butcher shop. Once I moved in, I cut back my work from full- to part-time. I'd come up with a plan to go back to school and finish what my father had prevented me from doing.

I enrolled in school and set out to complete the eighth grade. Admittedly, I was a little older than the other students—at sixteen, I should have been in tenth grade. But that part of it was all right. I was moving on in my life, and I felt proud of that.

What I didn't count on was how wiped out I'd be by the demands of the schedule. The school was an eight-mile bus ride from Lawrence to Methuen. Afterward, I had a full day of work ahead—hours of climbing ladders and laying tape and making sure I didn't mess up anyone's trim. By the end of the day, I was too wiped out to think straight, let alone do any homework. Eventually, this wore me down, and my desire to graduate from high school wasn't enough to keep me going. I chalked it up to experience and realized that school was something I'd have to put behind me. So in that respect I guess my father won.

Once I'd dropped out for good, I went back to work full-time. I began to make good money, too—about $265 a week. I got along well with Mr. Davis. That made going to work much easier. He treated me like a son, maybe because his own son, Ralph, was causing him so many problems and I seemed pretty responsible—and well-behaved—in comparison.

Still, there was a big difference between how Mr. Davis treated Ralph and how my father treated me. That became clear to me the day Ralph asked me over to his place for dinner.

I was so intimidated by the idea of sitting down with Mr. Davis and his family that I lingered in the doorway, unsure whether to come in. I'd never seen a house like it. Everything matched: The sofas and the chairs in the dining room matched. The silverware was a matching set, as were the napkins at each place setting. There was even a tablecloth. I'd never eaten a meal on a tablecloth before. Mr. Davis and Ralph's three brothers were already seated.

"Come on, Wayne, take a seat," Ralph said, motioning me to sit at the end of the table by Mr. Davis.

Then they bowed their heads and Mr. Davis said grace. I'd never experienced anything like this, either. A few moments later, Mrs. Davis appeared with a platter of meat in her hands. She wore a white apron and smelled like roast beef and gravy. But what was more astonishing was that she came over to serve me first! I was being served even before Mr. Davis. I couldn't get over it.

"Is that enough?" she asked.

"Yes," I said quickly. I was afraid if she gave me too much she'd run out and there wouldn't be enough for everyone else.

"Well, there's plenty more," she said, as if she was reading my mind, "so let me know when you're ready for seconds."

Seconds? I was just amazed.

The food smelled so good that I could have inhaled it all in one breath. Once again, I had to restrain myself to keep from wolfing it down.

The surprises didn't stop there. Mr. Davis began to ask his sons questions about how their day had gone. When Andy, Ralph's younger brother, sheepishly admitted that he'd gotten a D on a chemistry test, Mr. Davis slammed his fist on the table and said, "Damn it, you can do a lot better than that."

When he said that, I shrank back in my chair, sure that Mr. Davis would jump out of his seat, yank Andy out of his chair and beat him. But instead he went right on eating, although he was obviously upset. "You're grounded for two weeks—no car and no phone privileges," he told Andy, "and if you don't do better on your next test I'll ground you for another two weeks."

That was it. He never called Andy stupid or lazy. He wasn't going to hit his son. He'd grounded him and that was that. What's more, he did it to get him to do better the next time, not for any other reason. I was beginning to realize how little I knew about the world. How I used to think that everyone lived like we did, except that maybe they might have had a little more money. The beatings and abuse—I always thought that was universal, no matter how rich you were. Now I could see that maybe I'd been wrong. People actually lived like civilized human beings; they didn't necessarily mistreat each other. There were kids who didn't cringe in terror every time they heard their father walk in the door.

Strangers came around our apartment around the clock, often late at night. They'd bang on the door, demanding to see Ted. They never said what business they had with him, but I had my suspicions. One night I was watching TV with a girl I was dating, when there was a loud knock on the door. Three guys in leather jackets were standing there, looking impatient and agitated. "Where's Ted?" one of them demanded. It was clear to me that these guys didn't have Ted's best interests at heart.

"He's not here," I said.

"Well, where is he?"

"Look," I said, trying to keep my cool, "I don't know where he is. He doesn't live here anymore." That wasn't the truth. I thought Ted was in some deep trouble, and this was my attempt to cover for him. Then the guy said, "We're going to make you tell us." With that he sucker-punched me in the nose.

I hit the floor. My girlfriend shrieked and ran into the bathroom, slamming the door shut. I bounced right back up. And before the guy could punch me again I grabbed a hammer off the kitchen counter and went after him and his buddies. I was so incensed I didn't remember I was only wearing my skivvies. I just charged down the stairs after them and chased the three of them into the street. Seeing me with the hammer, tearing down the block, they must have figured they were dealing with a maniac. They scattered like flies, but I was interested only in the one who'd hit me. When I caught up to him he whipped around to confront me and tried to stab me with something; I think it was a screwdriver. Before he could, though, I hit him on the head with the hammer. He staggered back but grabbed me by my arm, so I was unable to get in a good swing to do any real damage. Still, I managed to give him a number of lumps on his head.

Then it suddenly occurred to me what I was doing. I was really hurting this poor guy. He wasn't putting up a fight. What was I going to do, kill him? I came to my senses. The anger just died in me like air spurting out of a tire. I stopped hitting him and said, "Dude, I didn't mean to hurt you. Come back to my place and I'll put some ice on those lumps."

He was so shaken and in so much pain that he didn't say anything. He just shrugged and let me guide him back. So after having nearly knocked him senseless with the hammer, I ended up taking care of him. I felt guilty.

"Look," I said to him, "I don't know what your name is, but you shouldn't have come in and punched me like that."

He nodded miserably, holding the bag of ice up to his head. "My name is Larry," he said.

Once Larry felt a little better, he and my girlfriend—who had come out of the bathroom by now—and I walked down to the corner bar, and I bought him a beer. He told me he used to belong to a biker gang, one like the Hell's Angels. I knew the gang he was referring to. It was a pretty big deal in the Lawrence area at the time.

That fight with Larry taught me a lesson, though it would be many years before I could fully absorb it: For all the rage I felt, there was another, positive force inside me. I just had to find the courage to let it come out.

Eventually, Ted really did move out. At first I was happy to have the place all to myself. I didn't have to worry about getting into hammer fights with late-night callers. But—with Ted's help—I was capable of getting into trouble, too, as I was soon to discover.

My downhill slide began on my sixteenth birthday. All the abuse and craziness of my life—things that I'd thought I'd left behind when I ran away from home—caught up with me, even though I didn't know it at the time. It happened at a big party I threw for myself. I invited everyone I knew and a lot of people I didn't—friends and friends of friends. Ted showed up. He drew me off into the corner. "Hey, Wayne," he said, "we really ought to celebrate."

I said I thought that that's what we were doing.

"No," he said, "I'm talking about really celebrating."

Then, with a furtive look, he took a bag full of white powder out of his pocket and showed it to me. He didn't have to tell me what was inside. I already knew. It explained why all those guys were always coming around asking for him. He'd been dealing drugs.

I was tempted but I was still going back and forth in my mind whether to try it. "I don't know," I said. I did some pot now and then, but had never tried anything harder.

"Just once, Wayne," Ted was nothing if not persistent. "Just to see what it's like. Aren't you curious?"

Oh, yeah, I was curious. I was very curious.

The first time I got high on cocaine I felt like I could do anything—hit on any woman, take on any job, charm anyone—better than anyone else. So I did it again, and it was just as good the next time.

At first I told myself I could control it. Just once or twice a week, I promised myself. I'd treat myself for a job well done, like a reward. The heroin was for weekends and maybe a hit in the middle of the week, to get me through. I figured that I was okay because I was still working most of the time. If I took a week off now and then it was okay. If I needed money all I had to do was show up and Mr. Davis would put me to work. I wasn't the only one who was doing drugs. Most of Mr. Davis's workers were on drugs or booze or something. None of them could be considered a dependable employee. Since his workers were calling in sick every day, Mr. Davis was always able to use an extra hand. So even if you didn't show up, Mr. Davis would still give you work the next time you were there. But I knew he was disappointed in me.

My life fell apart. I lived in chaos. My apartment was a mess. The ashtrays were overflowing. Remains of takeout dinners were strewn over the counters. I began to lead the type of life where there was no telling from one minute to the next what would happen. Anyway, I didn't care. The only thing in the world that mattered was getting the smack into my veins. Needles were everywhere—on the floor, on the bed, in the sofa. It had gotten so that I didn't even notice when I stepped on one. The only thing that mattered was the rush—the incredible sense of calm—that hit me when I pulled the needle out of my arm.

I was starting to lose it. I was getting heavily into drugs with Ralph, Mr. Davis's bad apple son. We began to hang out all the time. It was just a bad scene. One of my friends had died of an overdose. I didn't care. I didn't think I had much to lose. If I wasn't shooting up and getting high, I was scrambling around for cash to buy another nickel bag or waiting for the dealer to show up. Days could go by like that. I was the needle man.

Heroin gives you a mellow high. I used to whack up a bag of it and just sit down in a chair, slip some headphones on and listen to music. I'd basically veg out. Heroin became my whole life; I could only go for a few hours without shooting up. Like most heroin addicts, I had no appetite for food at all. The sight of it made me gag. If I did try to eat, I'd throw up.

Then Ralph and I began to experiment with a lot of different drugs. You name it, Ralph and I were doing it. We needed money to feed our habits. When heroin is your life, you'll do anything to get it. We sold watches, books, records, tapes—anything that might have any value at all. With a habit costing $175 every day, you constantly have to come up with new ways of getting money. When we ran out of things to sell or pawn, we began to explore other options. Ralph started stealing checks that he found in his father's basement. The checks were all bad, since they were drawn on closed accounts, but local grocery stores allowed us to cash them in, and we got what we could. We'd hit five or six different stores at a time and collect enough money to get us through a week or two. Work was a last resort, when we couldn't come up with any better idea to earn some cash. Ralph was a real smooth talker, a real con man. Occasionally he'd get somebody to front him and give him money. Of course, he'd never quite get around to paying the guy back.

It got to the point where we actually had to flee to Maine. We couldn't hang around the Lawrence area anymore because Ralph had burned so many people. Although Ralph was more involved in these scams than I was, I was certainly a willing accomplice. Plus I was cashing a lot of bad checks myself. I barely gave any thought to the consequences. As far as I could see, cashing a bad check was like walking into a bank but without a gun and mask and saying to the teller, "Give me your money." Inevitably, of course, the checks bounced. What I didn't realize when I was doing this was that I was being recorded by hidden video cameras in the banks. And all the checks we'd bounced were going back to Mr. Davis, so it didn't take long for him to catch on to our game.

By this point nearly two years had passed since I'd left home. My life was a complete shambles. But I was so far down that I was totally unaware of who I was or what my life was really about. I'd been in denial for so long about my upbringing that it was almost second nature to me to keep the blinders on. I'd just go along from day to day without ever stepping back and saying, "Hey, Wayne, what the hell do you think you're doing?" I wasn't questioning anything.

One day I went over to see Susan and my nephew, who was four at the time. Although my sister could tell that something was wrong—in a matter of six or seven months or so I'd gone from 160 pounds to barely a hundred—she never asked me what I was doing. It wasn't from lack of love—my father might have played his kids against one another, but we all still cared about each other. But we came from the same family, after all: Denial and lack of communication were key.

After saying hello to her and her kid, I excused myself to go to the bathroom. There was no lock on the bathroom door, so I just shut it and sat down on the toilet and started shooting up. I was so absorbed in what I was doing that I didn't notice when my nephew opened the door and stood staring at me. Susan was standing right behind him. The worst part was seeing the horror in her eyes.

Then I heard a voice and a chill ran down my back.

Is that her? I wondered. Could she be here or am I hearing things?

But it wasn't a hallucination. Ma was here. I hadn't seen her since I'd run away.

And now she was running, too—again. That was why she was at Susan's. I hadn't known that when I'd come in. Now I was exposed. My secret was out. When I stepped out of the bathroom, I found my mother waiting for me. She took one look at me and started to cry.

All sorts of things flashed through my mind then. I was astonished at how good it felt to see her after so much time had gone by. But I was also astonished about something else—her tears. Usually Ma went around with kind of a glassy look in her eyes. Only the latest baby got a lot of attention. So I was truly stunned—and through my humiliation, I was glad—to see my mother show that she cared as much as she did that day.

"Oh," she said through her tears, "just look at yourself, Wayne. Just look at yourself."

I was a drug addict, and my appearance, like my life, was a mess. I was also aware that I'd lost weight. To top it all off, I was in denial, as I had been my whole life. Looking in the mirror was something I hadn't done at all in the past couple of years. So when Ma told me to look, I wasn't sure what I'd see.

I went back inside the bathroom and gazed at the mirror on the door of the medicine cabinet. It took a moment for me to actually understand what it was I was seeing. But once I did, I was blown away.

My light brown hair hung in crusty strands around my face. My cheeks were caved in, and you could see the outline of my jaw and even my gums along my chin. Worst of all, my eyes were hollowed out, like I was haunted, and there were huge black circles underneath.

How had this happened? When I was a kid, I'd found a place within me where I'd be protected from my father. I'd promised that child in the mirror that no matter what, he would grow up and tell the world what had happened to him. I had a mission to fulfill. If I remained true to the mission, I swore, I'd always be able to find my way back to my safe place.

I didn't know when it had happened, what month or year, but somewhere along the line I'd forgotten what I was supposed to be doing with my life, I'd forgotten about my promise to that child, and I'd lost my way. Now I felt totally alone.

One by one, I went through all the official documents, but there was something I still couldn't understand. The MSPCC admitted that it had known about my parents' neglect for eight years. The doctors at Tewksbury Hospital concluded the same thing. So why, then, with all of this evidence and the opinions of doctors, social workers, and police officers, did the system turn around and hand us right back to our parents? They'd been arrested for neglect and abuse, and let out on $400 bail, which was a lot of money back then. They were obviously unfit to be parents. What conceivable justification, what rationale was there for the state to give them another chance to raise us? It was only when I got hold of a copy of the state records of our case that I understood exactly what had happened.

> The case of neglect against Mr. and Mrs. Theodore was heard in the Lawrence District Court by Judge Darcy. Upon hearing the testimony, Judge Darcy asked the social worker, Miss Poveda, to explain how she saw the situation. She noted the rapid improvement in home conditions by Mr. T. She felt that the parents deserved to have their children back in view of the desire expressed by the parents for another chance. Judge Darcy continued the case for six months . . . and placed the responsibility in the hands of the probation officer.

But the probation officer, Mr. Duenes, had a different take on the case. He didn't think that giving my parents a second chance would do any good. This was how the state put it:

After the court session, I talked with Mr. Duenes about the possibility of Family Service being used to help the family with financial management, care of the children, and dealing with some of the Theodores' personal problems. He said that he would talk to the people at the Department of Public Welfare about seeking such help, but he expressed his misgivings, since he didn't feel that the Theodores would be able to profit from this kind of state intervention. On the contrary, he said he felt that the same pattern of behavior of abandonment and neglect seen in the past would recur and that it wouldn't be long before the family broke down again.

It was as if the state was washing its hands of us. No one was going to monitor what happened to make sure that my parents weren't repeat offenders. The upshot was we went back to our fortified encampment in Methuen. At least we all stayed together. If we'd been farmed out to foster care undoubtedly we'd have been separated. The other side of the coin was that it got worse for us. Now, with the court breathing down his neck, my father had to be on his guard. He knew he couldn't do anything to mess up, or he'd lose us for good. You'd have thought that with all the problems—and expense—we caused him that he might have been just as happy to see us gone. But that wouldn't be like my father. The thing that ruled my father—more than anything else—was his sense of pride.

It didn't mean that he was going to treat us better if we came back, though. All it meant was that whatever he did, he'd have to be sure to do it in such a way that he wouldn't get caught again.

I left the Theodore household at fifteen, but escaping didn't allow me to shake my belief, deep inside, that I was worthless. All my life my father had pounded in a message with every blow. And it was a message more powerful than any pain his fists or kicks could inflict: *You're no good. You're worthless. You'll never amount to anything. You'll never have any friends. No one will love you.* And the worst part was that deep inside I believed him. Maybe that was how I ended up in such a rat hole, with a needle stuck in my arm.

It's one thing to realize that you should quit doing drugs; it's something else again to actually go ahead and do it. One day you swear you're never going to touch the stuff again, and the next you're shooting up like there's no tomorrow. And for a heroin addict, there *is* no tomorrow. But I couldn't get that day at my sister's place out of my mind. I had looked at myself in the mirror for the first time in a very long time and, no matter how I tried, I couldn't shake the memory of my face in the mirror, that little abused boy staring back at me through the eyes of the person I'd become.

Because I suspected that maybe my father was right, that I really was a worthless human being, maybe, I thought, I deserved to treat myself badly, too. It was obvious, even to me, that I couldn't make it on my own. I had screwed up royally. So I needed to be punished. I wasn't clear about this at the time, but when I think about it, I'm pretty sure that was why I went back home, and why, when my father raised his fist to me, I didn't resist. I was getting what was coming to me.

All the same, there was another part of me that was determined to quit drugs, start my own business, and live on my own again as soon as I could put enough cash together. How was I going to do that? I thought about it. The business I knew best was housepainting. So I picked up some brushes, put an ad in the paper, and before I knew it I was in business.

The first job I got was to paint a candy store. It was a good job, not too big for a beginner without employees. I didn't make any money, because I forgot to factor in the cost of the brushes or that it would take two coats, but I did the job to the owner's satisfaction. So I was off and running. I started hustling, and when I had a few more jobs lined up I contacted two of my younger brothers, who'd quit school to bring in money for my father, and asked them to come work for me. I didn't have any trouble convincing them, but when I told them that they'd have to wear white coveralls they looked at me like I was crazy.

"I'm talking about looking professional," I said. I took my cue from Mr. Davis, of course.

Things didn't work out exactly as planned. One time, one of my brothers didn't show up for a job; another time the other brother stole some valuables a contractor had left lying around the site. And I wasn't any better. I couldn't think; I couldn't talk to anyone. Giving up smack was proving much harder than I'd imagined. Soon I was back to shooting up. My hands were shaking so badly I couldn't apply the paint without spilling half of it. My voice cracked when I talked to clients. My legs wouldn't stop moving. My stomach wouldn't take anything but Coca-cola or beer. I was a mess.

Being on my own was exhausting, and I decided to take a break from it. At that time, being on my own meant being on drugs. I didn't have the discipline to break the habit by myself. And I wanted—*needed*—to break the habit. That meant getting away from Ralph, and it meant—at the time—moving back in with my family. I rationalized it every which way: I told myself my father was older and had mellowed; I was older and had lived in the world. This part was true: I couldn't very well do dope with my father around. If I'd done it once, I could do it again. I was no longer the scared little boy my father could push around. I was seventeen years old; I had some money; I had a business. I could walk out whenever I wanted.

I called Ma to tell her I was going sober. It was kind of a promise, though I still hedged a bit in my mind. The drug has so much power that it's almost like giving up a friend. Of course, it's a friend who doesn't have your best interests at heart, but you tend to remember only the good times you had with him. I could tell by the tone in my mother's voice that she wanted to believe me. At that moment, I wanted to believe myself. I told her I would stop by and see her. That was a big thing for me, because it meant going into the snake's lair, and there was no way of knowing, once I went back, whether it would be so easy to escape again.

I kept my word. It was getting close to Christmas. Mr. Davis came to my rescue and loaned me his car, even though I didn't have a driver's license. In spite of everything, he still had faith in me. I think now that it had little to do with me; it was just the kind of person he was.

Despite his drug habit, the guy that got me started on drugs—Ted— was not only a pretty warm guy, but still my friend. It was his suggestion that I buy everyone in my family Christmas presents—a new concept for the Theodores. It would help smooth my way back into the family. So with all this Christmas stuff to get done—picking out the tree, the decorations, the gifts—I could keep my mind off what would happen when I saw my father again. For all I knew, he might take one look at all the gifts I'd bought and throw them into the yard.

Home wasn't Methuen anymore. In the past two years, my family had moved to Derry, New Hampshire, fifteen miles away. It was quite a big jump for my father, deciding to come out of the woods after so many years. I don't know exactly why he moved, but my guess is that he had more money (after all, many of my siblings were working now, and still handing their paychecks over to him). And he'd already paid off the mortgage on the place in Methuen. It was almost as if he'd decided to become a little more civilized. Or maybe he just hoped that people would see him as the big shot he imagined himself to be.

For my big homecoming, Ted came along with me for moral support. When we got near the house, we parked some distance away, because I didn't want my father to see the car. You never knew what would set him off. Then the two of us dragged the Christmas tree out of the back and started toward the house. I figured if he came at me I could use the tree as protection.

My mother, wearing her usual big billowy dress, opened the door for us. As soon as she saw the tree, she clapped her hands in delight and called to all my brothers and sisters to come have a look. Everyone crowded around me. I was like a conquering hero. Then I got the gifts and began to distribute them. My father just stood there. He didn't do anything to ruin the show. He seemed strangely calm. But while I was relieved at how well my reception had gone, I wasn't fooled. If he was acting friendly it could only mean that he wanted something from me.

The question was what.

My father was in his early forties by now. After having been away for almost two years, I had a little distance, and I began to notice things about him that I hadn't before. He wasn't the all-powerful figure I remembered. Far from it. I'd see him trip over his feet or catch him fumbling when he tried to pick something up, and I'd think to myself, he has absolutely no coordination. It occurred to me that he wasn't a very strong man, either. He's not tall—about five feet six inches—and he seemed even shorter to me now that I'd grown a little taller. He has a stocky build and large hands, but most of his power back then came from another part of his body—his mouth. He was still getting into fights at local gin mills to prove himself a tough guy, but they weren't really fistfights. He wasn't a man who'd go toe-to-toe with anybody. He'd wrestle, and pull the ultimate low move—he'd clamp down with his teeth and bite, hard. *That* was how he had to win.

He'd bought a new home and had some money in the bank. The house was different, and my siblings' clothes were cleaner, fit better, and had fewer holes. Even their shoes seemed to fit. They ate better food than when I'd lived with them—the moldy bread was still around, but as my siblings had grown old enough to work, they ate more protein and drank more milk and soda.

Shortly after I came back home, my father announced his plans at dinner. "I want to buy a 'dozer and start my own business," he said. Then he passed me a plate of fried chicken and told me to help myself.

Now, I thought, I'll find out what he wants from me.

I was right. He turned to me and added, like it was an afterthought, "I need you to help me pay for it."

I didn't answer him right away, but did some quick mental calculations. My father was not a good businessman: I figured I could more than double his earnings. If I helped him buy his bulldozer—and other equipment he'd probably need—it would give me leverage. I knew that, if I was to going to make my life tolerable there, I'd have to do some negotiating. I had to settle things up front and make it clear to him that I was on an equal footing with him, that he couldn't treat me the way he had before I'd left home. At least that was the plan.

"All right, Dad," I said, "I'll help you buy the 'dozer." During the next couple of days, we worked out a deal. I told him he'd make more money if I went back to work on my own, housepainting. After all, my business was already established. What was the sense of giving it up to go to work directly for my father? This way he'd be making money from two businesses at once—his own and what I threw him out of my income. The dollar signs were dancing in his eyes.

"You and I are going to be partners," he said.

Partners! That was a new one. But it was fine with me: My father would be in debt to me—right where I wanted him.

There was no question who my employees would be. My father told my brothers—five of them—to work for me. The pay was the usual going rate for the Theodore kids—that is, next to nothing. The plan was for my father and I to split the gross. Then he'd dole out a few bucks to my brothers and pocket the rest. He went one step further and paid my brothers different amounts. It was a variation of his old divide-and-conquer strategy. He was setting a trap for them. Michael would admit that he was getting thirty dollars, only to find out that Christopher was making seventy-five. That caused a lot of resentment.

My father was unconcerned. "If they don't do what I tell them to do they're dead," he told me. His rule was that if one of them didn't work like a slave, I was to tell him, and he'd take care of it. He'd beat them to death. He was the Mafia. He was doing the same thing he always did, trying to play one brother against the other.

I pretended to go along with him, but I had other ideas.

I'd give him enough money to keep him happy, but I wouldn't cheat my brothers. How would he know how much I gave them, as long as he got his share? One way or another, I figured, I'd still make out all right. He wouldn't find out.

My painting business began to really take off. It wasn't long before my brothers and I had made enough cash for our father to buy both a bulldozer and a trailer to move his machines from one construction site to another. My father was happy, and why shouldn't he be? He was making out like a bandit. I was giving him a thousand to fifteen-hundred dollars every week. But the more I thought about it, the more I felt it was unfair that my brothers weren't getting what they deserved: The pitiful handouts my father was giving them didn't go far, so I began paying them each an extra fifty to seventy-five dollars a week in cash. Just don't tell Dad, I pleaded with them. They said of course not; why would they rat on me when I was paying them extra? I hoped for the best. They, like me, had been bred to be tattletales, and my father still had a lot of power over them.

The beatings stopped. My father was a lot of things, but I have to give him credit—he was at least sharp enough to realize that if he beat my brothers he might get carried away and put them out of commission for a few days. He didn't want to risk losing an employee. And, since I was the person who was putting the whole thing together, he knew enough not to touch me at all. At least that's what I thought.

I had another advantage over him. My father had no way of knowing how much money my business brought in. In theory, we were supposed to bring home copies of our contracts and proposals along with the names and phone numbers of the people who had hired us. My father even insisted on seeing the empty paint cans from each job so that he could check to see whether we'd done as much work as the contract specified. Although all the checks coming in should have gone directly to him, I managed to intercept them. In any case, I wrote up contracts that indicated one price for the client and fake contracts that said something different for my father. So I was giving him the shaft, but I wasn't losing any sleep over it; it was just a little extra work.

I was in no hurry to leave home. I had sobered up. Business was going well, I didn't have to pay rent, and I was saving up some money for myself. I was content in my routine. Things were looking up.

My father—who in the meantime had launched his bulldozing operation—must have figured something was up. One day, about two years after I'd moved back in with him, he announced he was changing our arrangement.

"From now on your brothers are going to work for me and not you," he said. "I need them more than you do."

What's more, he said, he expected me to keep my business going on my own so his money would continue coming regularly. It didn't seem to occur to him that I wasn't going to be able to make the same amount of money working as a one-man operation. But I didn't see any sense in arguing. What would have been the use? My brothers would do whatever he said, so I relented and told him he could do what he liked. And while I kept my business going just as before, I had no intention of forking over half my earnings to him. In any case, he was kind of losing track of what was going on, because now, with my brothers gone, no one was watching me.

One night when I got home from work at around eight o'clock, I walked into the garage and saw my father. He looked like he'd been waiting for me for a long time, and the look on his face was poisonous. I'd seen that look a thousand times before, and it meant I was in big trouble.

Without saying a word I turned to go. He came after me and grabbed me by the hair. That was the worst part, because he had his fingers woven into it, yanking at it just like the "derooting" he'd given my sisters when they were little. He dragged me into the driveway and began to kick me in the head, the chest, my stomach.

It had been years since he'd attacked me. I'd known he was mad, but I hadn't seen this coming. I was totally off guard. At first I wanted to hit him back. I was really ready to explode. But I held back. I told myself, *Relax. Just take it. You'll get even.*

So I did; I took the beating. It was the same kind of beating he used to give me when I was a kid, except now it no longer hurt. I was bigger; he was weaker; and what's more—he didn't matter to me as much anymore. I wasn't as vulnerable.

"What the hell did you think you were getting away with?" he yelled.

I had no idea what he was talking about.

"The paint cans, you moron! I counted!"

Now I understood.

"I want to see all the receipts! You're going to give me all the goddamn receipts for your jobs! You didn't think you could get away with pulling this shit on me, did you now?"

I later found out that he'd confronted Michael and demanded to know what we'd all been doing for the last several months. And he'd made Michael talk, the usual way—by pounding him until he admitted that I wasn't giving my father his cut.

Of course, my father was stupid to think counting the paint cans would do him any good—no more than checking my receipts would, because he didn't know how much any particular job was paying to start with. (The fake contracts I'd drawn up made sure of that.) So the number of paint cans didn't make a difference. Still, he had to punish me and make my brothers think he could figure out our scheme. There was nobody better, nobody smarter, stronger. The message was always, *Don't even try it. I'm the boss. I'll beat you every time.* The incredible thing was that this indoctrination worked for so long.

It hit me like a thunderclap. *I'm not afraid of this guy.* The fear had vanished. It was like you've been sick for weeks, and then one day you wake up and think, *Something's different.* You realize the fever's broken.

This bastard is a weakling. He's a coward. Why hadn't I seen it before? I'd always thought he was the ultimate strong man. I'd always thought he was unbelievable. But having been out in the world a little bit, I'd gotten smarter. The blinders had been removed, and at last I could see my father as if I hadn't known him all my life, as if he were a complete stranger.

I'd come so close to hitting back, but I'd talked myself out of it. Why hit back? That would hand him the victory he wanted. My father was feeling so inferior, so insecure and powerless, that he didn't know any other way of venting his anger and frustration than by hitting and kicking and biting.

But that wasn't me. *No,* I thought, *I'll hurt him another way.*

I was a little scared, but mostly I was angry. We were supposed to be business partners, and partners are equal. Partners don't beat each other up. The best thing to do, I thought, would be to leave tomorrow and never come back. That way he'd get no money from me at all.

I didn't give him any hints. To appease him, I said he could have three-quarters of my pay. "From now on, Dad, I'll show you all the contracts and receipts."

"Okay," he said. His shoulders sagged a little and he looked at me a little sheepishly. "You know, I feel bad, I really do. I shouldn't have hit you, Wayne. You're a good boy."

You're a good boy.

The next day I was gone.

For the next two years that I was on my own, I reveled again in my freedom. I found an apartment and began to build a contracting business. New jobs were coming in, and I was making some nice money. I had a girlfriend. I seemed to be off drugs for good.

But if I thought that the past—and my father—no longer had a hold on me, I was dead wrong.

You relive it in your mind. You go over it again and again, thinking about what you could have done differently. If only you'd made the turn a minute or so before you did; if only you'd paused a few seconds longer at the stop sign. If only you'd been paying a little more attention to the road and weren't so lost in thought. So many if-onlys. . .

It happened so fast I didn't even have a chance to be scared. There was a squeal of rubber, then a thud and a shriek of metal. Then silence.

I just sat there for a while. It was as if time had come to a stop. At first I didn't know whether I was hurt. I didn't seem to be bleeding, but my relief didn't last long. I looked over at the car I'd just smashed into and saw that half the chassis was crumpled in. The window on the driver's side was shattered. I could make out the head of the driver through the jagged gap, but he didn't seem to be moving.

All sorts of thoughts went through my mind. Maybe I'd killed him, or maybe he was so badly injured that if he didn't get help right away he'd die.

I climbed out of my car. The front end was banged up, the hood had popped open, and steam was coming out. It looked pretty bad.

My nerves were shot. My legs were so wobbly I could barely keep upright. People were gathering across the street, pointing and staring.

What lousy luck, I thought. An hour before, I'd been barreling along the highway, thinking how sweet life was.

Just don't let the guy be dead or paralyzed, I prayed. I can't have that on my conscience. I wasn't even sure whose fault the accident was. I didn't see him coming. I was probably going too fast.

Then I detected some movement. The driver of the other car was struggling to get his door open. When he stepped out of the car I felt a surge of relief. He looked pale and shaken, and no wonder, but otherwise he seemed to be in one piece. No blood. He could still walk.

And he came out of the car shouting at me. "What are you, *blind*? What's the matter with you? I had the right of way."

I didn't really know what to say. "Look, man, I'm sorry. I didn't see you."

"Tell it to the cops." Then he demanded my name and number and the name of my insurer.

"My insurer?"

"Yes, jerk, your insurer. I need to know your insurer. Who's going to pay for the damage you've done to my car?"

I just stared at him.

"Speak up. I can't hear you."

"I don't have any insurance," I said.

What I didn't realize, though—not until later anyway—was that I hadn't just totaled a car. I was now out of money and couldn't afford to live on my own. Because of the accident and the hole it left me in, I realized I'd have no choice but to go back to work for my father. Which meant I'd lost my freedom, too.

So at the age of twenty I was back home. Home had changed again in the two years I'd been away. Now my father—with his new business doing well—had settled our family in Londonderry, just down the road from Derry. He'd moved up in the world; now he had a small ranch-style house with an attached garage. He was a little older, a little mellower, and living in—compared to our beat-up house in Methuen—more style. But he was as stubborn and strange as ever, and this was his newest rule: The house was off-limits to everyone except Ma and himself. Nobody else could go inside, except to go to the bathroom. The house was like a temple, and we weren't allowed to worship.

Amazingly, this meant packing everyone else into the garage, a space twenty-two by twenty-two feet, with a concrete floor, no carpeting, no room dividers, no living-room sofa—nothing at all like your "typical" home. When I got there, we totaled fourteen people, including my grown siblings. Some of them had new families of their own—like Joseph, his wife, and their new baby, and Michael and his new wife, Joanne. My sisters-in-law—patient women, both of them—simply accepted it as part of their new lives. In a bizarre way it felt comfortable and familiar: In Methuen our windows had been covered with plastic; in this new garage, you also couldn't see in or out, because my father had ordered my brothers to paint the windows over. It was a typical family situation for us. We had total privacy from the outside world, but zero privacy from each other.

For heat and cooking we used a wood stove that stood in the middle of the concrete floor. For furniture we made do with a round wooden table; we sat on the floor to eat. The TV was our only luxury, and my brothers ran the cable from the house into the garage. We parked the cars outside on the driveway. When I think back, it's ridiculous that any of us—especially the newlywed couples—put up with it.

But the weirdness didn't end there. My parents didn't sleep in the house either. They, too, slept in the garage. My father's bed was a cot, and my mother slept on the love seat in the breezeway next to the garage door. Everyone else claimed a spot on the floor and slept under old blankets. None of us had a pillow. The bathroom for the boys was the woods; the girls could use the bathroom in the house.

By the time I moved back in my father had all his boys working for him. His setup worked this way: He rented out his bulldozer at a discount—twenty-three dollars an hour instead of the going rate of thirty-five—and as a bonus he threw in four laborers—my brothers. It didn't cost him extra, since he never paid them a cent. On the other hand, my father—who wasn't exactly great at customer relations—didn't come out making the kind of money he should have. There's no other way to put it—he was a terrible businessman.

He put me to work running a backhoe. He gave me room and board and fifty dollars to work a full forty- or forty-five-hour week. Fifty dollars! When I think about it now, I can't do anything except laugh. Fifty dollars was slave wages, so I was a slave who was still in debt. He kept me down, and in doing so kept me in sight.

But the positive side of me—the one I discovered the day I stopped myself from bashing a guy's head in with a hammer—kept me strong, and nudged me along. Deep inside, I knew that someday I would regain my independence. I may not have known then how, but I was sure it would happen. With that in mind, I kept saving my money, and I took odd jobs on the side—housepainting here, running a tractor there. Then, like an idiot, I took another really bad turn.

My first mistake was getting married.

I'd had a number of girlfriends on and off over the years. I never had any problem finding girls. The problem was holding onto them. There was a woman who lived just up the street from my parents' new place. Ronnie was a slender brunette with a taunting, tempting look in her eyes. Ronnie had been thrown out of her parents' house for going with too many guys, just like Ma and her parents years ago. When I met Ronnie, she was looking for a place to crash. I offered her my car, and she took me up on it.

Ronnie and I fell into a relationship pretty fast. Because she had left home and was sleeping in my car, she reminded me a lot of myself the summer I was fifteen, when I spent every night in that old Buick. She was great fun to hang out with, and she wasn't afraid of anything. And she was pretty sexy. And I made her laugh.

Progress can be so slow it's almost imperceptible sometimes. But by this point—at the rate of fifty dollars a week plus the money I got from the odd jobs—I'd managed to save up enough to strike out on my own again. It would be my third time hitting the road. This time when I left home it was no big deal. I didn't have to escape; I just told my father I was leaving. I was a grown man, and he didn't try to stop me.

When I thought of being a grown-up, I imagined having a steady paying job, a woman, and a house. I was old enough—twenty-two—to want all that, so I made it happen. In my case, the house was a trailer I bought with the money I'd saved. The woman was Ronnie. Together, we chose to anchor the trailer in Salem, just a few towns away from my family in Londonderry.

My relationship with Ronnie was rocky from the get-go. At first, the good times were good; we had our laughs together. But the arguments got longer and more out of control.

We hadn't been living in our new home for more than a few months when Ronnie told me she was pregnant. When Ma heard about the pregnancy, she said, "You better marry this girl. I don't want to see your kid being born without a father."

I wasn't in love with Ronnie, and, looking back, I knew it then. On the other hand, I wanted to do the right thing.

We didn't have a big or fancy wedding. It was in a small church in town, with a few friends and family members from each side. On the day of the wedding I got roaring drunk. I staggered through my vows, with Ronnie—who had a bad temper—shooting me poisonous looks the whole time. Once the pastor pronounced us man and wife, Ronnie grabbed her veil off her head and stormed out of the church in a fury.

I was genuinely confused, not to mention more than a little wasted. Was I supposed to run after her, act nice, and lure her back? Or, if I did that, would she start taking me for granted? Should I teach her a lesson? I wasn't planning on beating her up or anything, not like my father did to Ma all the time. But I thought about hitting her a few times. I hated the idea that she would walk out on me in front of my friends and family, on our wedding day.

Having wanted this, I was suddenly clueless about marriage in general, and how to deal with my new, grown-up life.

You think you've got a handle on your life, and then you come across another point of view, and you suddenly realize that your version was full of big, gaping holes. The court report on my family's case had that effect on me. There were many revelations in the report, but one thing threw me completely—something I'd never suspected.

"When Wayne was placed with his grandparents, his buttocks were rare. . . ."

That's how it begins, like I was a piece of meat. It's a pretty good description. At first, I had to laugh.

It goes on:

On 10/10, 10/14/, 10/15 [1958], when a social worker visited, the father was present. He attempted to dominate the conversation; whenever the mother said anything the father would tell her to shut up. He wanted the child placed immediately—the next day Wayne was ready; a complete outfit had to be bought for him. He was taken to a foster home.

A foster home? What was this? I was given up for adoption? The other reports had only referred to the Theodore children being removed by the state from my parents' custody. But this was the first time I'd seen a report that only mentioned me. And in this instance it wasn't the state that was intervening. I went back and read the words again. But I'd gotten it right the first time. From what I could see, my father wanted to give me up, on his own. Not my brothers and sisters. Only me.

"The foster mother cleared him of cradle cap in several days. Wayne loved lying in the bassinet in the kitchen watching the other children, and the activity in the home."

I remembered nothing about this—I was too young—but I can imagine that even as a baby I'd have picked up on the difference between my new home and the chaos and violence in the one I'd come from. In my new home there were no beatings. That must have been an amazing change for me.

But the vacation didn't last long. "On Oct. 30," the report says, "Wayne was returned to his parents' home." No explanation.

Why was I put into foster care to begin with, if my parents turned around and took me back? That was something I couldn't figure out.

But I was a tireless detective, and I pieced it together. I remember one of my older siblings telling me that, just before this time period, Ma had walked out on my father. She had said it was for good. See, the timing was the key. My mother had left my father on October 2, and eight days later he was giving me up for adoption. It seems like he'd wanted to give me up all along, but her presence had stopped him.

Then my mother came back, and I was removed from foster care and returned to my parents. I could only assume that I had had something to do with their big blow-up. After all, it wasn't as if my parents were giving up their other kids. I was the only child my parents were voluntarily agreeing to place in foster care. It seemed I'd been a bargaining chip, the price my mother demanded from my father for coming back to him.

About two months into her pregnancy, Ronnie lost the baby. The miscarriage was pretty dramatic—one second she was crying out in pain, the next she was on the floor and blood was gushing out of her. I couldn't help thinking about Ma—when she'd had her miscarriage such a long time ago—and what my brothers and sisters and I saw when we peeked in the toilet.

I felt bad for Ronnie. I tried to be a good husband, tried comforting her. But it did cross my mind that the reason we'd gotten married was no longer there. There was a lot of drama; Ronnie had a way of pushing my buttons. She'd get mad at me for something I thought at the time was pretty minor, like staying out late drinking with my buddies. Instead of talking about it calmly, she'd just get angry—the way she had at the wedding—and run out of the house, knowing I was going to run after her. And I always did. Sometimes she'd walk out in bare feet with no coat, even when there was snow on the ground.

But we were married, and neither of us considered splitting up. After a few months, Ronnie wanted to try for another baby. I wondered whether this was the right thing to do, but I did what people do when they don't have any vision in a relationship. I thought having a kid might be a good idea. It might help make our relationship work.

I got my painting business going again. I saw money in contracting, too, and this time around I hired some guys to do that, too. Business was good, we were getting jobs, and soon that fifty dollars a week seemed like a distant memory. The rest of my life might have been out of control, but things were different when it came to work. I could throw myself into it and block out everything else.

I already knew how to do all sorts of jobs, but now I was learning to supervise them—running bulldozers and backhoes, grading roads, laying sewer lines. I combined the work so a general contractor wouldn't have to go to a bunch of different subcontractors. And it paid off. I always got a job done on time, and usually I came in under budget. Customers liked me; workers liked me. On any given day I could find six, ten, twelve guys who were ready to come and work for me the next day. I hate to brag, but that's no small achievement when you're new to the business and in your twenties.

I was competing with my father. He was still running his business with the help of my brothers. But, as I knew all too well, working for my father was a trap, and my brother Michael soon realized that, too. When Michael wanted to buy a small Toyota pickup truck, my father offered to co-sign a loan. My father had established sufficient credit with the local bank, which had financed his house, but it wasn't as if he was doing this out of the kindness of his heart. By co-signing the loan, he was keeping Michael tied to him. That was clear from the way my father arranged the deal. Michael never made the payments to the bank directly. Instead my father took the money out of his pay, and *he* dealt with the bank. This way he kept Michael in hock, keeping most of the money for himself, while putting a little aside for the car payments and giving Michael whatever scraps were left over.

One day Michael had had enough, and he told my father he was quitting. I don't think Michael would have made the decision on his own initiative. It was mostly his wife's doing; Joanne was tired of watching my father berate and humiliate Michael. Besides, she was infuriated that he was being paid only a pittance. She took it for about a year, and then she went to my father and said, "I'm not going to let you abuse my husband anymore."

My father was livid. It was bad enough when one of his kids tried to challenge him, but he sure wasn't going to take any grief from a daughter-in-law. After that there was no turning back. He was determined to make Michael pay, so he went to the bank and told the loan officer that Michael was no longer making his car payments to him. This wasn't true, but the bank officer had no way of knowing that. So now my father said he needed to repossess the truck. The loan officer agreed to transfer the title of the truck to my father, depriving Michael of any legal right to it.

Not only had my father taken Michael's truck, making it harder for him to earn a living, but he'd also ruined his credit—and Michael was only eighteen. And that wasn't all. Once the banker had agreed to his terms, he turned around and gave the Toyota to Brian. Basically, he was pitting one son against another. He split those two brothers apart like night and day. Michael never forgot it.

I asked Michael to come work for me. Things changed fast for Michael after that; instead of having to settle for the scraps my father threw him, he was pulling in four or five hundred dollars a week. That was very good pay for the time. After work, he and Joanne would regularly drop by our trailer and hang out.

One day my father showed up at my trailer with my mother in tow—a surprise visit. Joanne spotted them from the window and stepped out onto the porch. This was the first time she and Michael had seen my father since he'd repossessed the truck, and she was blazing mad.

"How could you do that to your own son, take his truck away like that and give it to his brother?" she shouted.

"Shut your mouth, you slut!" my father hollered back.

At this, Michael came out of the trailer. "Don't you call my wife a slut!" he screamed.

When I stepped out the door, I saw that my father and Michael were standing toe to toe. Then my father jumped him. Joanne swept down off the porch and was yelling at my father to stop. My mother just stood there, staring into the distance like nothing was happening.

I didn't hesitate. My father was in my territory now. This was my home. I just grabbed hold of him and tried to rip him off my brother. It was the first time in my life I'd ever touched him. I didn't think about it then, it all happened so fast. It was only later that I realized I'd crossed an important line.

But before I could pull him off he clamped his teeth down on Michael's back, as if trying to chew off as much skin as he could. I pulled harder and finally managed to get him off before he could take another bite.

My father didn't even seem to notice me. He was so charged up about Michael that he kept running his mouth at him. His face was crimson. His eyes were glazed. It was as if he were in a trance. He was in fight mode, and when he got like that there was no reasoning with him. It seemed like all he wanted to do was pound Michael into the pavement. I wasn't going to allow that to happen, so I put myself between them and broke the fight up.

Joanne came over and pulled Michael's shirt up so everyone could see the damage my father had done. There was a raw purplish mark on his back, and if you looked close you could see the imprint of the teeth.

"Look what you've done, you son of a bitch!" she yelled.

I was incensed. I took a look at my father, and I said to him, "You're an animal, biting your own son like that. You get the hell out of my yard. I want you off my property!"

"What did you say?" He had a look on his face like he was going to come after *me* now.

I took a step toward him to show that I wasn't afraid of him—not anymore. I put my hand out like I was offering it to him to bite.

"Come on, do you want to bite me? Come and bite me. I'll knock your goddamn teeth out."

He couldn't believe what he was hearing. His mouth fell open. He was so surprised that I'd confronted him like this, that he was struck dumb.

He didn't take me up on my dare. I just wanted him to come and bite me. I was giving him his opportunity. Here's a guy who'd been beating me up since I was a baby, and he wouldn't stand up to me. He knew what he was up against now. And he knew my reputation. He'd seen me come home with my face pounded in from getting into fights with some very tough guys. He knew that I'd stood up to them—guys *he'd* never fight with—so I was waiting for him to try something. I kept my hand out, waving it in his face. I really wanted him to do it.

He hesitated for a couple of seconds, and then he just sort of shrugged, turned around, and walked away. For years I'd known he was a coward, but now I'd seen it with my own eyes. He headed back to the car with my mother trailing after him. He was walking away with his tail between his legs, cursing me under his breath. That was what he was reduced to.

It had taken me twenty-three years, but I'd done it. My father was scared of me. And I'd proven to him—and, finally, to myself—that I was stronger. So this was what it felt like on the other side of the line, I thought. I could hardly believe I'd stood up to him. For years he'd tried to break my spirit and put me in a place where he could be the boss, and it hadn't worked. And now I knew—and he knew—that it would *never* work.

These days, I think of how important touch is for me. I touch my children, my friends, even my business associates. I hug my relatives and good friends. I can remember a life where my only experience of touch was pain. Even now, when I think of touching my father, I get scared. You can't be scared of someone for so many years and leave it behind completely. I try to imagine the courage it took to reach out and touch the untouchable. Pulling my father off my brother changed my life.

Before long, Ronnie was pregnant again. She'd been pregnant twice and miscarried both times, so I knew not to get my hopes up. Miraculously, this time she gave birth to a baby boy. He was premature by about a month, but the doctors were optimistic.

I was so happy. My first-born son. I had it in my head how I was going to teach him: He'd be a good man; he'd be proud, strong, and independent. He'd never fear his father; he'd never know hunger; he'd never be abandoned. He'd never know how it felt to be abused. He wouldn't go through what I had. I was going to give him a good life.

We named him Wayne Jr. Aside from knowing that I'd never take my fist to him, I had dreams for him. I wanted to give him everything I never had. I'd give him the world, if I could. And I don't mean just material things.

I was the happiest man alive—for a few weeks.

He was too small to leave the hospital. Because he was premature, he needed special care, so he was kept in the ICU. There were tubes running in and out of him, but I thought, okay, it's going to take some time, but he'll come out of it; he's doing really well, and soon we'll be able to take him home with us. Meanwhile, I stopped by the hospital every day.

But Wayne Jr. *wasn't* getting better.

We had new doctors to deal with—specialists of one kind or another—once it became clear that his condition wasn't improving. There seemed to be some sort of problem, and they began to do tests to find out what it was.

Finally Ronnie and I were called into an office. The doctor fumbled with some papers. He said, "Your child has a disorder called hyaline membrane disease."

I'd never heard of it. Hardly anyone else had, either, the doctor explained. But it was a condition not uncommon in premature infants whose lungs hadn't had a chance to develop normally before birth.

"Well, what happens now?"

The doctor went on to tell us what our options were, how they were going to see what they could do about expanding the baby's lungs. He said we shouldn't be overly worried. And I wasn't, because I could see for myself that Wayne Jr. was improving every day.

One morning, while I was in the ICU visiting my baby, a woman came up to me. She was in her forties and had a warm smile. She wasn't really pretty, but there was something about her that I liked.

"Hi," she said cheerfully, "I'm Elaine Crowley. I'm a social worker here." She glanced at Wayne Jr. and said, "This is your son."

It seemed she was familiar with the case. "I want you to know something," she went on. "If you ever just want to talk to someone. . ."

"Talk?" I said, "Talk about what?" I was dumbfounded. No one in my entire life had ever come up to me and asked me to talk about whatever was on my mind.

"I'm here if you need me," she said. It was as if she wanted to be my friend. Wow, I thought, she really feels for me and understands what's going on.

I probably wouldn't have been so elated by her offer if I'd thought about it some more. Hospital social workers, after all, are there to counsel parents with children who are at great risk of dying. There's nothing worse than sitting there helplessly, watching your kid die. But I didn't want to think about that. My kid wasn't going to die. My kid was going to get better. I could see it for myself.

All I could think about was that I'd made a new friend, that now I had someone to confide in. Whenever I was at the hospital, I'd look for Elaine. I was happy to talk to her about anything at all—it didn't always have to do with my baby. I don't even remember what I said to her. The only thing that mattered was that she was paying attention; she just sat there and listened to me. It struck me that no one had ever listened the way she did, ever. No one had ever cared enough to want to find out what I was feeling or thinking. No one in my family. Not even Ronnie. Ronnie was lost in her own world, always had been. It was such an incredible experience for me. I was stopping by to talk to Elaine so often that I apologized for taking up her time.

"It's all right, Wayne, I'm here for you."

Then all of a sudden one day my baby started to do really badly. I walked into Wayne Jr.'s unit and found several doctors gathered around him. It took a while before I could get the story from one of the doctors. He motioned me outside into the corridor.

"It's his kidneys," the doctor said. "They've failed. We're doing everything we can." He added that there were other problems, as well—that other organs were failing, too.

It wasn't just his words. It was his tone of voice and the way he was looking at me, as if he saw right through me, that told me just how things were. I stood there, facing him, not knowing what to say.

He asked me if I had any questions.

I shook my head.

I went back into the baby's room. The nurse said to me, "I don't think you can see him." When I protested she shrugged and said. "Well, you can see him, but you'd better brace yourself. I don't think he's going to make it through the day."

"I understand. Can I just hold him? I've never held him before."

She hesitated for a moment. She could see what I was going through. Then she said yes. At that moment, a doctor came into the room and he and the nurse began to talk. It was as if I were invisible to them. I walked to the other side of the room. Wayne Jr. was stretched out on a table behind a curtain. My poor baby was hooked up to a monitor and a life-support machine. There must have been a half-dozen tubes or more snaking out of him. He had a hose down his mouth and tape on his nose. You couldn't even see his face. His head was as big as a balloon. His body had inflated, because his kidneys had failed and the fluid was building up inside of him. I couldn't believe it. I was horrified. He'd looked okay only the night before.

I looked at him and I talked to him in a low voice. I said, "This machine is keeping you alive here. You're not going to make it. There's no way." I peered behind the curtain. The doctor and nurse were still talking, paying no attention to me. I knew how the monitor worked. I knew how all the machines there worked. And I knew what I had to do.

I shut all of the machines off. Then I pulled all the tubes out of Wayne Jr.'s mouth. I'd never seen his face without all the tubes and tape. I wanted to see his face at least once. Then I scooped his frail little body up in my arms and held him close. And he died in my arms.

The sudden silence alerted the nurse and the doctor. They rushed over to me.

I said, "I just wanted to see what he looked like before he died. I had never seen him without this tube down his throat."

The two of them stood there for a few moments. Then they nodded. They understood.

I had never felt so alone in my life. I didn't really love my wife, but I loved that baby. Now that I look back, I know I had high hopes for him, but he also seemed like kind of a solution for me—an easy answer to some of life's biggest issues. It was a little unrealistic. I'd expected the baby to change *my* life, but I know now that I'd have to change my life myself.

I left and went downstairs and out into the lobby. At that moment, I wasn't even thinking of notifying Ronnie that Wayne Jr. had died. I was in too much of a daze.

I found the nearest bar and sat down and proceeded to do something numbing—get good and drunk. It probably took no more than an hour to do the job. I was still drunk when I went back to the hospital that night. I desperately needed to talk to Elaine, but she wasn't available. I wasn't about to leave, though—not yet. There was one more thing I had to do.

I wanted to see my baby for the last time. I learned from the nurse at the reception desk that they'd taken him to the morgue. I said I wanted to see him.

She looked at me with astonishment. "Why would you want to see him?"

"I want to see him because I want to make sure everything is okay."

She seemed to expect me to say something more, but there was nothing more to say. I went down to the morgue, and had my closure.

I fed alcohol into my system all night long, so the next day I was still drunk. I was in a fog. I didn't know what I was doing. I had no idea where I was supposed to go. All I knew was that I couldn't stay where I was. Ronnie was crying. She was in pain, but there was nothing I could do for her. I left home. I got in the car and drove. I drove for two days. I might have gone around in circles. It didn't matter. I was so lost. I felt like there was nobody there for me—not a soul.

Then I realized I had to pull myself together. There were things to be done. I had to have a funeral for Wayne Jr. If I couldn't keep him alive, I could give him a decent burial. My father's family, I knew, had a plot available in a cemetery near Methuen. My son was only a baby; I just needed a small spot for him.

I went to see my father and said, "Look, I'm going to have a funeral for my baby and bury him."

I didn't know what I was going to do if he said no.

But he just shrugged and said, "Yup, you can bury him over there, no problem."

There were certain papers we had to sign that authorized the transfer of the plot. Once that was done, I thought everything was settled. But then I heard that my father was going around town bragging about how generous he'd been. "If it weren't for me that guy wouldn't have a place to bury his kid," he boasted, as if this "kid" weren't related to him.

I gave him a place to bury his kid. There was nothing he gave me with one hand that he didn't take back with the other.

(Years later, when my father was mad at me, he even went so far as to threaten to dig up the casket and throw my son out of the cemetery. I told him, "The day you do that is the day I'll kill you."

I know I should have been used to his callousness, but I still couldn't get over how heartless he could be. Did he hate me that much? What had I ever done that could account for the loathing he had for me? To threaten to dig up my son's body like he was a piece of garbage? There was something about me—more than any of my brothers and sisters—that gnawed at him, that put him into a mindless rage. He would never make peace with me. There must be some explanation. I had only wanted his love, and all he'd ever shown me was the back of his hand.)

There was still something I needed to do before I could say good-bye. On the day of the funeral, I brought a windup teddy bear with me. Back in the hospital, I'd stood over my baby's bed and watched his eyes brighten when I wound it up. I wanted him to have it now. I opened up the tiny casket, wound up the bear, and placed it inside.

And so we buried my son.

People I've talked to about it have told me, "Your baby was sick. It was probably the best thing that could have happened to him. If he'd lived, what kind of life would he have had? You wouldn't want him to suffer." All this is true—to a point. After all, he was only six weeks old when he died; it wasn't as if he were six years old. I'd hardly had a chance to know him. But I couldn't explain to these people what his death meant to me. This little boy was going to do something for me, and I was going to do something for him. And now that opportunity was gone.

kept thinking about Elaine. I was more anxious to talk to her than ever. The day after the funeral I went to the hospital to see her, and I started to tell her what this little boy had meant to me. Yet in telling her about Wayne Jr. I began opening up to her just a little bit about myself, too. I was trying to get a feel for what it was like to be honest with someone, to come clean about the past. But I was afraid to say too much. So much was building up inside of me that I was ready to explode, and I didn't think she could handle it. I wasn't sure I could, either. I was starting to reveal things about my childhood—things I'd never told anybody before. I was beginning to break the silence. I barely glanced at her the whole while. I was putting so much trust in her that I was afraid to meet her gaze because of what I might see.

I called her the next day to say that I wanted to see her again; there was so much more I needed to tell her. Now that I'd begun to open up I couldn't stop.

There was a strange silence on the other end. Then she said, "Well, your son isn't here anymore. I can't bring him back, and there's really nothing more I can do for you."

"What do you mean?" I couldn't understand how she could brush me off like that. "I've been opening up to you."

Maybe, I thought, she didn't realize that was what I was doing. She had no idea how important my talks with her were for me.

When she rejected me like that, I felt as though she'd almost trapped me, forced me to tell her things I shouldn't have. I felt as if she'd betrayed me. Hadn't she said, "I'm here for you"? I'd thought she was my friend.

I looked at the phone and was about to say, "Wait a minute now, I trusted you."

Then I realized that I hadn't made any deal with her. She never said she'd be my friend. That deal was all in my own mind. *I'd* made the deal.

I can trust you. I'm going to trust you.

But now I saw that it had never meant much to her.

"Wayne," she said, putting an end to our conversation, "I can't help you anymore. There's nothing I can do for you."

I felt hopeless and full of rage. I told myself, "Never again will I open my mouth; it's not worth it." There was nobody out there for me. I'd been about to break the silence, and I'd been rejected. So I went back into that silence. It felt like the silence was all I'd ever know.

needed to know more. I needed to get all the information I could about my childhood so I could put every last piece together. I became a full-time detective for a while. I went to all the schools I'd ever attended and asked to see my records. I can't say I was expecting much— just report cards and attendance records. But I didn't want to let any shred of evidence slip by. As it turned out, I overturned something big.

I sat in my pickup truck outside Pleasant Valley School—the place where Mrs. Cole had taught me to read and write. I sat and read through the yellowed paperwork. I turned a page in a file—and sat bolt upright.

The face of a little boy stared up at me. It *was* me, at six, in the first grade, a skinny, freckled boy with big hazel eyes and a determined look. On the back of the picture, all it said was "Wayne." There were so few pictures of me as a kid that it was startling to find this one.

I'd forgotten that the school arranged for class photos to be taken every year. My father never paid for any, but one year the pictures came free of charge. This was that year, and this photo was my one childhood souvenir.

I stared at it—hypnotized. For a second it was a little ticking time machine. *Was I that skinny? I was good-looking, though. Too bad I didn't know how to flirt with the girls back then.* At first I was really excited, but after a while I started to feel a little suffocated. It was making me uncomfortable. I looked around. It wasn't summer yet, so the weather wasn't the reason I suddenly needed to open the window.

The words came to me in a whisper. An accusation. *Where have you been? I'm the boy in the mirror.*

Suddenly, I frowned, almost violently. The muscles in my face twisted into something really powerful—something I'd felt only once or twice before. I fought it, but a feeling rose up from my stomach into my chest and shoulders, and I had to let it take over. A huge tear squeezed its way out of my eye and down my cheek, followed by another, and then there was a sob that was audible, and then another. They were tears of incredible, painful loss, like the tears I cried for Wayne Jr. when he died.

The boy in the photo was six years old, just like the battered boy who looked in the mirror so long ago and swore to get revenge. This picture would have been taken in the same year my father almost killed me, the same year I found the child in the mirror. Had I been true to that boy, or had I abandoned my responsibility to him? I was afraid of the answer.

The tears slowed down, and the sobs got quieter. After a moment I began—like a crazy person—to talk to the photograph. Out loud, after I shut my window. He knew most of it already, but I started from the beginning and told him my story—*our* story. I talked about everything that had happened to us over the years, and together we wondered what a different childhood might have been like. What would it have been like to laugh and play in your backyard, and not have to cock one ear always listening—and dreading—the sound of your father's tires up the gravel road? What would it have been like—when you wet your bed—to have your parents tell you it's all right, and just wash the sheets without another word?

No one can hurt you now, I promised. I had a new purpose—a special responsibility to him, that came from my long-ago promise. *I'm back on track now,* I told him. *Now that I've found you again, I'm not going to desert you.*

I said it again, coming to grips with it. My hands were shaking. On that day, I really started to understand what denial was, how much I'd been blocking out all these years. But not anymore. *I am not going to rest until I keep my promise to the boy.*

It occurred to me that the boy was helping me, too. He gave me meaning, a purpose, something to strive toward. We were in it together, him and me. He'd always been a part of me, and now, at long last, he was coming out of hiding.

Even though our marriage was a shambles, Ronnie still wanted a child, and she got pregnant again. This time she delivered a healthy baby—a girl we named Becky. But Becky—like Wayne Jr.—also was premature. She weighed only three pounds. She fit into my palm; she was so tiny I almost didn't dare breathe on her for fear of what would happen.

And unlike Wayne Jr., Becky made it. Soon she became my whole world.

My hope that somehow a child would save our marriage, though, turned out to be an illusion. We were still fighting, worse than before, but there was a difference now because of the baby. I'd raise my hand to Ronnie, and then I'd take a look at the baby staring at me with her big eyes in fear, and I'd feel sick inside. I didn't know what was going on. I was in the dark about what to do. So every time Ronnie would start screaming at me, the only thing I could think of was to leave the trailer and go for a walk.

After all this time together, Ronnie knew better than ever how to push my buttons. With the baby there, it was even easier. Ronnie had always been a runner, running away all the time, just like my mother had. But with Becky around, Ronnie would grab her—knowing how important she was to me—and disappear. Then I'd be up all night searching frantically for her. When I'd finally find her, I'd beg her to come home. I couldn't stand it if I couldn't see Becky.

Things went from bad to worse. I stumbled into the trailer one night and Ronnie was standing there with her eyes blazing. She'd been drinking and sitting up waiting for me for hours. The longer she waited the angrier she became.

"Where have you been, Wayne?" she demanded, "Why were you out so late?"

I'd had a long day at work, and I didn't need to come home to this. "Be quiet, you bitch!" I yelled.

Then out of the corner of my eye I saw her pick up an ashtray and fling it at me. I ducked and it flew by me.

I was so incensed that I grabbed her by the hair—just like my father did to my mother, my sisters. I yanked—hard.

Then Ronnie hit me and I smacked her back. The blow was hard enough to send her reeling and she fell against the wall. She reached up and took a glass of water from the table and threw that at me, too. It crashed into my elbow and shattered on the floor.

I took a few steps toward her, ready to hit her again.

"Come on, you bastard, fight back," she taunted me.

I stood there, frozen. I couldn't move.

Then I stopped. It struck me that I was ready to do exactly what my father had always done—beat his rage and anger out of his system. I didn't want to become my father. I couldn't allow that to happen. This is a *woman*, I thought, a human being, flesh and blood. You hate your father—he's your mortal enemy—and here you are becoming him.

The words came at me from somewhere inside my head. They were cold and clear, and echoed around my brain. Just two words.

Stop. *Now.*

I looked at Ronnie. She was still slumped against the wall. My hand was still in the air as if I were about to hit her. I turned and walked out of the trailer.

From that moment on, I never struck a woman again.

The whole time my marriage was falling apart, I blamed Ronnie, not realizing what was really going on. How could I? It would have meant coming to terms with my past. I didn't understand that I was carrying all the weight of my whole life on my shoulders. I didn't connect the breakup to what I'd gone through growing up. It just didn't occur to me.

Several weeks after the incident with the ashtray, Ronnie left me, taking Becky with her. She went to live at her grandmother's. She was doing just what my mother used to do. But I refused to do what my father had done; I didn't run after her and beg her to come home. I didn't even call her. The marriage was over.

Ronnie and I saw each other off and on after the initial breakup. I think we both hoped that we could somehow make the marriage work. During that time, we had another child together, a boy we named Jimmy. I was thrilled to have a son. Although Jimmy never lived with me, I loved him and had high hopes for him. Ronnie and I couldn't make the relationship work and eventually we stopped seeing each other, but my love for my two kids never wavered.

One beautiful spring day a few months later, I stopped off to use a pay phone at a Laundromat in Londonderry. As I made the call, I noticed a pretty brunette taking her clothes out of a dryer. I guessed her to be about sixteen or seventeen years old. It turned out she was working there part-time. I was so distracted, I stopped listening to what the person on the phone was saying. She must have sensed I was looking at her, because she got self-conscious and looked away.

I hung up the phone, took a deep breath, and went over to talk to her. She was shy—I learned that her name was Sharon, but not much else. She had a sweet smile and big eyes, and, looking at her, I wanted to tell her everything. So I watched her fold her clean laundry, and I spilled my guts to her. Right there in the Laundromat. I told her what I did for a living. I told her I was separated from my wife, with a baby girl, and that I supported both of them. While I was telling her all this, I wondered if I was telling her too much. Even if she was interested, why should she want to get involved with someone who was married, with a kid? Had I gone too far? Was I scaring her off?

I still don't know why Sharon got to me the way she did. I suppose I had a feeling about her. Have you ever walked through the front door of a house you've never been in before, but you suddenly felt at home there? I guessed that, in spite of the awkwardness, she was just a teeny, tiny bit interested in me, too. I asked if I could take her out on a date. She hesitated. I braced myself for a *no*. I wouldn't blame her—after all, there was really nothing I could offer her.

"Okay," she said.

I looked up. I could hardly believe my ears. "What about tonight?" I'd probably stepped over the line there, but I was afraid that if I gave her too much time to think about it, she'd change her mind.

She hesitated again. "Okay," she said. "But I live with my parents. So I can't stay out too late."

"Where are we going?" she asked when I picked her up that night.

"No place special. We'll just drive around."

I had a surprise in store for her, one I was thrilled about.

"This car is dirty," I said. "It needs washing."

So for our first date we went to the car wash. She sat in the car while I lathered the chassis with soap and vacuumed the upholstery. The whole time she kept looking at me as if she was trying to figure out what I was all about. I knew what she was thinking: *Who is this guy? What am I doing with him? Why has he taken me to a car wash?*

After the car wash I took her back home. "Hey, do you want to go out tomorrow?" I asked before she could open the door.

She gave me another look like: *Do you think I'm crazy?*

Then she shrugged. "Sure," she said.

I wasn't surprised by her answer, but she certainly was.

She later told me that her parents had strong objections about her seeing me. "You're dating an older man who isn't even divorced yet, with a kid—and a reputation," her mother reminded her.

When Sharon protested that, once you got to know me, I was really a nice guy deep-down, her mother muttered something about how her daughter understood nothing about men.

But as much as she defended me to her parents, Sharon still had her doubts—and why shouldn't she? I was pretty unusual, after all. I'd grown up in a fortress-like encampment, and used the woods as my bathroom. I'd had only seven years of education. I'd never really celebrated any holidays, not even my own birthday. I was getting over a divorce. And I wasn't sure I knew how to love.

I was crazy about her. I felt I could be myself with her. I'd lost so much in my life that the possibility that there might be someone there for me was amazing. Was this the person who could finally understand me? I was pinning all my hopes on it. I called her ten times a day—asking how she was, how things were going. I guess I was insecure, because I was falling for her and I didn't want to lose her. I'd lost so much already. I was afraid that maybe she'd forget me and meet someone else and not love me anymore.

Week after week I sent her flowers—bouquets, long-stemmed roses by the dozen. Even her mother had to admit she'd never seen anything like it.

"What does a girl have to do to get all this attention?" she asked Sharon.

"Go out with Wayne Theodore, I guess," was her reply, typically casual.

Still, her mother remained convinced that I wasn't the right person for her daughter. She told Sharon that she wasn't to see me anymore. "Don't expect to stay in this house if you keep going out with him."

But she underestimated her daughter's will. Sharon refused to drop me. Instead she moved out and found a place of her own.

We continued to date. It wasn't perfect: We fought, we left each other, and we came back together. Finally, after five long years, we decided to get married.

When I think back now, I realize how much of an adjustment Sharon had to make to put up with me. In my early twenties, I was still a cocky teenager, hot-tempered, always primed for an argument. I was oversensitive and quick to blow things out of proportion. And I was impulsive; I'd see something I wanted—a snowmobile, a new car, whatever—and I'd be ready to spring for it whether I had the money or not. I liked to go out with the guys at least once a week, leaving Sharon alone. I didn't want to be pinned down as to what time I was coming home.

Sharon accepted me with all my faults. It was a pretty big thing for me to meet someone like her. I didn't know how big, at the time, but when I look back on it, I realize it was another huge turning point. I trusted her. I loved her. And because I loved her, I started to give her little bits and pieces of my life. I told her about my father's daily beatings. I told her that I used to live in fear of his every step, in fear of anything I might do to set him off on a rampage.

Sharon couldn't relate to any of this from her own life—her parents were caring people, with only her best interests at heart—but she didn't have to. She just listened to me, nodding every now and then. More importantly, she empathized.

Just to be able to get it out was so incredible—the weight it took off my shoulders. I felt lighter as I walked around. I was less hyperactive, less anxious.

But for as much as I shared with Sharon, there were things I didn't reveal. You couldn't find it if you had X-ray vision. Sharon couldn't see it, and I'm not sure I could either.

Denial is a powerful thing.

was ready to make something happen. I wanted to do something big. I'd taught myself a lot about painting and the excavation business. I knew how to lay a sewer line, how to calculate a grade, how to line out a road. I had a good business reputation, and that counted for a lot in a close-knit community. I'd repaired and renovated houses, and I understood the contracting business better than anyone out there. Now I felt I was in a position to take the next step. I was going to build houses.

I decided to go into business for myself. Why should I take orders from other people and let them profit? I had the experience, I had the track record, I had the reputation. I might make a mess of my life, but when it came to working, I'd proven myself time and again. So I just said, *Boom. This is what I'm going to do today. I'm just going to go out there and rent a truck and a bulldozer and find some workers and begin this thing.* I was incredibly motivated.

I had a few disadvantages, though. I had no high school diploma, no formal vocational training, and no credit history. After all, I'd never made any car payments. All I drove were old junkers I bought with cash. For that matter, I had no record of regular employment. I didn't own a typewriter, a briefcase, or a suit and tie.

I knew I'd have to apply for a loan. I had something big in mind, just to get started—on the order of over a half-million dollars.

I talked to a builder I knew. "What do you think about the idea of combining excavating and construction?"

"Impossible," he said. "It will never work."

That cinched it. I'd do it. The new me was confident, the new me knew no bounds, the new me didn't accept concepts like "can't" or "never." This business idea was a solid one; it could be done. Getting there was simply a challenge, no more: I'd make it work. I hadn't known how to drive and I learned as I'd gone along. I hadn't known how to survive, either, and I learned how to make that work, too. What I wanted to do now was going to be a damn sight easier than what I'd already done.

I had the chance to prove myself when a developer I knew gave me a contract to build a house for him. The house would be built on a subdivision. Here was the opportunity I was looking for. I walked the land and imagined where the house would stand. I saw in my mind's eye the way the road would go and how the sewers would be graded, laying it all out step-by-step in my imagination. I knew I could become a developer, too; I could build a whole subdivision—several subdivisions. But before I could do anything I needed to get a loan.

Even after I was given the name of a banker, it took me a few days to work up the courage to call him. To my relief, the banker didn't brush me off. He patiently explained the procedures I had to follow to apply.

It took me months to put together the blueprints and financial statements and fill out all the forms the bank wanted. The night before I was to meet with the banker, I paced back and forth in my bedroom, rehearsing what I was going to say, psyching myself up for the big day.

As important as the meeting was, though, I wasn't going to try to pretend to be something I wasn't. That morning I put on what I'd usually wear—T-shirt, jeans and work boots.

I went into the bank, telling myself that I was going to do okay. I knew I could do it. I spread out my blueprints on a table in front of the bank officer and did my dance. I told him about the vision I had for the subdivision. I described what the houses would look like, and I tried to give him an idea of the kind of people I believed would want to buy them. By the time I was through, I'd painted a picture of a thriving community that so far existed nowhere but in my wild imagination.

When it was over I turned toward the officer for his reaction.

"I'm impressed with your presentation," he said. "I'll take it to the loan committee to review your application, so it will probably take a few weeks before I have a decision for you."

I left the bank, feeling nervous and exhilarated. As I stepped out into the parking lot, I spotted a new Mercedes sitting there that made my heart soar. "Someday I'm going to buy a car like that," I promised myself.

Two weeks went by without a word. Then another week. I was beginning to get worried. How long would I have to wait?

I was sitting in the kitchen when the call came. When I hung up I turned and looked at Sharon.

"What's wrong?" she asked.

I reached out and grabbed her and spun her around the room. "Get out the champagne, Sharon," I said, "I've got the loan!"

It had taken a long time—six years—but I finally made my dream happen. Or that's what it seemed like to me. I felt like I was on top of the world. The business I'd started—the one I might have believed was "impossible" and a "stupid idea"—had grown into a big success. And I'd done it all by myself. I'd begun with next to nothing and had fought my way up the ladder. By working my hardest, I'd built my contracting business into a company worth several million dollars. I was proud of what I'd done. After six years, I could drive around southern New Hampshire and northern Massachusetts and see houses I'd built, land I'd developed, sewer systems I'd installed, and roads that I'd graded. I learned as I went along, because the truth was I really didn't know what I was doing until I was doing it. Common sense built my business. Other people doing the same kind of work had gone to graduate schools and gotten degrees in engineering and business to do what I was doing, and I had a seventh-grade education.

I'm not famous, I don't entertain people with singing or movie directing, I haven't invented a cure for cancer, and I don't lead governments, but I make my own kind of contribution, and I wanted the world to recognize it. So I decided to build another house, a special house, something that would blow the other houses away. And the house wouldn't be for a customer—it would be for my family and me.

It was going to be a big house—4,600 square feet—and it would be set on a hill surrounded by oak trees. In the back I planned a deck and a pool and a three-car garage. I designed it with the idea that it would be just the opposite of the house I'd grown up in, in Methuen. Instead of being hidden or fortified, my dream house would be there for all to see, on an open sunny clearing just above the road. The view from the site was spectacular. You could look across the road and see mountains rising over the tree line. This house, I resolved, would tell people how far I'd come in my life. It would represent my pledge to make a good life for my wife and our three little girls. With my history, I might have ended up in jail. Instead, I'd be living in a million-dollar house.

One night, just after the foundation for the house was laid in, Sharon and I decided to celebrate our good fortune. We drove out to the construction site with a bottle of chilled wine and sat on the ground in the spot where the chimney would rise someday. Then we watched the moon come up, and we made a toast to our new house. It was one of the happiest nights of my life.

But it wasn't long before everything began to go to hell.

Filled with dreams of the future, I built the house. In the winter of 1988, Sharon and I and our three young daughters moved in. Four years passed. For a time, everything went well.

In the late eighties, the economy began heading south. Contracting jobs were drying up, and my business was nowhere near immune to this. I felt things spinning out of control.

For years I'd been honing my ability to tap into the positive side of my personality. And I applied my positive outlook to every situation imaginable, including the current downslide. I figured the economy couldn't continue sliding forever. I wanted to hold onto my house, to my lifestyle, which allowed Sharon to stay home and the girls to have a decent upbringing. But the truth was, I was headed for financial ruin.

I'd lie awake nights, running the figures through my head. I'd think about a job I'd just put in a bid for. *If it comes in, it'll cover the mortgage for next month. After that, surely something else will turn up.* But then the job would evaporate. Maybe the bank wouldn't spring for the financing, or the project was delayed. It was always something.

In 1992, I finally threw in the towel. I was running a three-million-dollar business, but I had debts totaling two million dollars, and my creditors were starting to breathe down my neck. I filed for Chapter 7 bankruptcy. For months, I didn't even want to get out of bed.

I was thirty-five years old, and my business, which I'd founded and nurtured over the years, had failed. I'd hit rock bottom. That may sound strange, considering all the beatings I endured as a kid and all the other things—my runaway mother, being raised in a prison environment, being broke, running away, heroine addiction, having to move home time and again, my poor dead son, the loveless first marriage. But in a lot of ways, this was worse. I think it was because this business was mine—mine alone—and I had no one to blame for its failure but me.

Getting rid of the house was the most depressing part of it. I loved living there, I loved looking out the kitchen window into the backyard, at my baby girls playing. After I filed for bankruptcy, Sharon and I had to move out immediately. For two years, we rented it out. After six years, we had to put it up for sale and say good-bye to it for good. I consoled myself, thinking, *Well, okay, Wayne, you don't actually have to own the house, in some way it's still yours. You built it. It doesn't lessen your achievement.*

I was in mourning for my business. Whenever I talked to someone about what had happened, it was as if I were talking about someone close to me who'd died. I kept trying to think of ways to salvage it. I'd dream we were all back in our house and there was money pouring in, only to wake up in the morning and realize it was all gone.

I was just wandering around like a sleepwalker, going from one day to the next, not really conscious of what I was doing. I'd be talking to someone and in the middle of the conversation I'd realize I had no idea what was being said. I was very depressed. I was up one day and down the next. I had two modes: I was either hyper or sulking. People didn't know where they stood with me. I could be laughing and kidding around, and then suddenly, for no apparent reason, I'd lash out or fall into a funk and want nothing to do with anyone. I didn't even want to have anything to do with my three daughters, whom I knew I should love and support even if they couldn't have everything I wanted to give them.

I've always had mood swings. But before, I was in control of my highs and lows. They didn't interfere with my life. Now I knew I was losing control. And I knew the reason, too: I was blocking every possible positive force in my life. I went around telling myself I was a loser. And what's worse, I believed it.

Sharon and I were at the bottom of the barrel. With all the financial strains and my erratic behavior, it was no wonder we weren't getting along well. The smallest things set us yelling and screaming at one another.

But she wasn't to blame. I knew most of it was my fault, that I had to straighten out the mess. So one day I went to her and promised I would get my act together. Sharon cried, and looked lost and vulnerable. I almost felt like I was making up to a child; maybe I was making up to the little boy I used to be, who still lived inside of me somewhere.

"Our marriage is so very important to me," I said to Sharon, "I'm going to make this work, I'm going to change." Then, when she didn't say anything, I went on, "I know I need help. I know I can't do it alone."

This was a big admission for me, because for years, ever since I'd left home at fifteen, I was determined to make it on my own. I kept telling myself that I didn't need anyone's help. But after what I'd been through, having lost my baby, my business, and my self-respect, I could see things had to change.

As I was making my promise, Sharon looked at me as if she wanted desperately to believe me, but I could see she needed more than words.

What I didn't know was that, while I was going through this mourning period, a lot of other things would happen that would turn my life around forever.

The calls were nonstop. While I was wrestling with my business problems, my brothers and sisters had problems of their own, and I was the one they spilled their guts to. A couple of my brothers were reaching their late twenties and, like Brian, they were questioning their behavior and mood swings. One of them complained about wanting to strike out and hit someone when he was upset or frustrated; another worried about feeling a sense of hopelessness at least once a day. A third brother told me that whenever he looked around him, he felt like the rest of the world was filled with people who knew where they were going and were happier than he was. He felt completely out of place.

They opened themselves up to me, and I was glad. It was obvious they looked up to me, and not just because I was always the "brother with his own business." I think they saw my positive side, and they hoped I could help them. I love my siblings—I always loved them, even when they ratted on me when we were kids—but I had too many problems of my own to deal the right way with theirs. So for a long time, I just listened, tried to give a little advice, and left it at that.

Then I got the call from Brian—the one that started my investigation into the past. I thought about that call, on that cold winter day.

"I know you can help me," Brian had said.

Out loud, I'd promised Brian I would help him. But at the same time, I made a silent promise to my other brothers and sisters: *I'm going to help you, too.* And I made a silent promise to myself. I had every intention of sticking to my word.

Once I'd gathered all the information I could find—the reports from the state authorities and the Massachusetts Society for the Prevention of Cruelty to Children, the newspaper articles, the school files—I got ready to use it.

It was time to fulfill my promise to the child in the mirror. I wanted to tell others about my horrible childhood, about what my father had done to our family. In part, I decided this out of love for my brothers and sisters; I couldn't see any other way for them to come to terms with who they were unless they came out of denial, like I had, and confronted our past. But to be fair, it was also for me, to make more progress on my long, bittersweet journey.

Telling has power. I knew that because of the look in my father's eyes—and because of his fury—every time the school found out about something he did. I knew it because of the way he acted to people who weren't part of his family, like that doctor in the hospital I went to when I was three. I knew it because of his threats to my mother about what he would do to her if the authorities ever came knocking on our door again. Even before I was sixteen and my father hunted me down at Susan's to shut me up, I knew that exposure—or telling—was one thing I could be sure would really, really rattle him. What went on in my house when I was a child was still officially one big, fat secret.

But the chains of my father's threats and intimidation no longer held me back. Now I could give information out freely.

Telling might get my father into deep trouble. Even if he didn't go to jail, he'd lose his dignity. And I felt that, if nothing else, my father needed to lose his dignity, so the rest of us could start to heal.

First, though, I had to know what the law was, whether my siblings and I had the right to take any action against him. I contacted the state district attorney's office in Massachusetts to find out about statutes of limitations, but the assistant district attorney I spoke with more or less blew me off. After he'd heard my story, he told me he'd have to look into the matter and get back to me. Maybe he was really busy, but I never did hear from him.

There might have been other people at the district attorney's office who could have helped me. But this man, this assistant district attorney, was as far along that road as I wanted to go. After he failed to call me back I decided to try other options.

I got on the phone with my brothers and sisters. "I think we all need to sit down and talk," I said. "I've got some papers to show you."

"What kind of papers?" they asked.

"You'll have to wait and see," I said.

So we all gathered one night in my living room. I'd made copies of all the documents I'd been collecting for the last several months—documents they'd known nothing about—and passed them out.

I sat down and watched their expressions as they read. Some of them were quite devastated, as I was.

"This isn't true," said my youngest sister, Linda. Her face was drained and she was shaking her head. "You're making this up." But even as she said this I think she knew that it had to be true. It was all there in black and white.

"It happened, Linda," I said as gently as I could.

"Jesus, I didn't remember ever living in Massachusetts," said Kenny, one of the youngest. "But now I do. I remember it now. Not clearly, but I remember it."

That was how they all were. Some of the younger kids were like Kenny—they'd been babies or not even born when the events described in the papers had happened. But the older ones had pushed the memories so far in the back of their minds, buried them so deep, it was as if these things had never happened at all. Or they'd convinced themselves the abuse hadn't been that bad. Or it could be they'd felt like me, that they'd been punished deservedly, that my father hadn't done anything a million other fathers didn't do all the time.

In other words, although they sensed that the reason their lives had gotten so screwed up was because of what had happened to us, they still couldn't quite put two and two together. They still hadn't come to terms with the idea that they'd suffered, and that we'd all been robbed of our childhoods, because they were taught to think that they were nothing, that their lives had no value. They didn't really know what they'd lost.

Now I was making them deal with the past in a way that was threatening to them. And they had no choice, because I was presenting them with objective evidence—reports from social workers, court decisions. This stuff was impossible to deny. Seeing their past laid out for them in black and white like that was an incredible revelation for them.

I told my brothers and sisters how important it was for us to tell the world what had happened; revealing the truth was our only option. I wanted the whole world to know what he'd done, and once the secret was out, we could be free. What choice did we have? We couldn't live in silence forever. We couldn't live in shame for the rest of our lives.

I realized that by involving my brothers and sisters, I'd made a large commitment. I'd assumed responsibility for catching them as they fell onto the other side of their painful past. As soon as I'd exposed them to the truth, they were in my care. I knew who they were. I knew what they'd gone through. And even with all my troubles, I realized that I was probably the strongest one.

"So what do we do now?" Brian eventually asked.

Everyone was still trying to come to grips with what they'd just read.

We needed to get our story out; everyone was in agreement on that. But how? I'd been playing with an idea, and I threw it out there.

"What about going on one of those shows—Oprah, maybe, or Sally Jessy Raphael?" I said.

"We'll never get on Sally," Michael said pessimistically.

But of course, I never take "never" as anything but a motivation to make something happen. I was sure we could do it if we really wanted to.

At first, none of my brothers and sisters took it seriously, because they didn't believe going on a national TV show was even possible. But the more we talked about it the more it seemed like it could happen. The feeling was that we had nothing much to lose by trying. Nobody objected. I think most of my brothers and sisters thought that, if they did

go on a TV show, they'd become stars. That was why they were so enthu-
siastic—not because they thought, as I did, that it might be a way to
resolve the problems in their lives. They had visions of making bundles
of money from Hollywood. But I wasn't going on that show to become
a superstar. I just wanted—I needed—to straighten out my act.

Convincing my siblings seemed easy, but now came the hard part—
getting on a show. I didn't want people to think of us as a freaky sideshow
act. I wanted to do something that had more meaning. It was a very, very
hard thing to do, to go on national television and tell the world all our
secrets. But taking such a decisive step would mean a lot for my brothers and sisters; it represented a big commitment on their part, because
once we made our appearance there'd be no turning back. If we'd kept
the truth to ourselves, it would have had no power, because it would let
our parents off the hook. But by letting the world know, our parents
couldn't escape the truth—and neither could any of us.

Together, we wrote a letter that touched on all the basic points: We
were twelve siblings who had been treated violently by our father growing up. As teenagers, we'd been forced to quit school to go to work. We'd
just learned that when we were little, we were abandoned—not once, but
twice. We were all in various stages of denial, and to break out of it we
felt we had to tell our story. The letter was short, but we promised that,
if we were chosen, we'd all go on the show.

We overnighted copies to a few popular daytime talk shows. Then
we waited.

The answer came immediately. When I came home the next day I
found a message on my answering machine from a producer at the Sally
Jessy Raphael Show. I called back and filled her in on the kind of story we
had in mind, including details I hadn't mentioned in the letter. I made it
clear that I wasn't out for revenge. That wasn't my intention. What it came
down to was a way for me to be free, to finally begin to heal.

The producer sounded interested. "I think we might have something
here," she said, and she promised to get back to me with a definite answer.

The next morning, when the phone rang, I had a feeling about what
was going to happen.

"Wayne," she said, "I've discussed your story with Sally and we want
to go ahead with it." She then named a day a few weeks away when they

wanted to have us on. "After hearing what you've told us we're all really excited about this," she went on. "We'll do whatever we have to do to get you here, but we want all of you here on this show."

So I'd been right. I'd been sure we had something powerful to share with the world, although I don't think the producer truly realized at that point what they had. For that matter, I don't think *I* really understood what we had.

A few days later I got another call from the show. The same producer got on the line. "Look, Wayne," she said, "Sally and I have been talking it over and we would like your mother and your father on the show with you."

Something in my throat coiled shut. "No way," I said, "absolutely not. It will not happen." Doing this was already a big leap; the thought of doing it in front of my father made me want to gag.

"Well, how about if we talk to them?"

"No, you better not," I said. I didn't even want them to know we were going to be on. "I want them to turn on the TV and see us," I said. "I don't want my father to have a chance to hide under a rock."

The producer was insistent. She and Sally had decided that the only way the show would really work would be for my siblings and me to confront our parents' behavior in front of them. We—and the audience—would have the benefit of seeing their reactions to our pain, and possibly experiencing forgiveness.

"Suppose I give you a picture of my father and you put that on the air?"

"No," she said, "we can't put his picture on TV without his consent."

She was waiting for me to propose some kind of solution. Finally I said, "Okay, let me work on it."

I've got to figure out how to do this, I thought. Maybe I could get them on the show, after all.

There had to be some way to get my parents to appear on the show. It would be tricky, but I was sure I could pull it off. The question was, how?

By this time, Ma had finally escaped my father's clutches for good: The two had been divorced for eight years. Every time I thought about it I was amazed. After all, she'd left him so many times and had always come back. And maybe she would have stayed with him, too, but it helped that she moved to Florida first, and then found another man to marry. Pretty soon, she wasn't taking his calls any more.

In terms of getting them on the show, I came up with a strategy, and believe it or not the strategy came from my father. He lived in New Hampshire, and she lived in Arizona, and there had not been a word between them for a very long time—years. I'd use my father's proven strategy—divide and conquer. After all, no one ever said he never taught me anything.

I started with my mother. I flew down to Arizona to see her. She came to the airport to greet me in one of her trademark billowy dresses. She was cheerful and smiling, as always, but I thought that this time there was a less distant—and a little bit sharper—look on her face, especially when she saw the big manila envelope in my hand.

She made us coffee at her house, and we sat down at the kitchen table. I didn't wait to deliver the punch. As soon as I sat down with her I pulled out the news clippings about their arrest and gave them to her. I didn't want to show her everything; I held back the big guns. I was acting dumb, pretending I didn't have all the information, but what I gave her had its desired effect. At first she just looked puzzled, but when she saw the headline "Case Continued" her jaw dropped. She seemed about to say, "What do you want from me?" but she stopped herself. She couldn't believe I'd found out. "You told me there was a charge," I said innocently.

I was nice about it, but I had her cornered, and she knew it. I was forcing her to face a truth she'd tried desperately to avoid all these years. But she reacted just as I'd expected. She began to accuse my father of being responsible for all the bad things that had happened.

"I loved you kids, I would do anything for you, you know that, but he wouldn't let me. He would have killed me if I'd tried to stop him. I was afraid for my life." She was getting really worked up, practically hysterical. Exactly what I'd expected.

"You know, Ma, everybody's blaming you for this." In fact, I was the only one who believed that she was as much at fault as my father. "Everybody's starting to see you as the bad guy. Do you realize that everybody in this family—all my brothers and sisters—are, wondering why you left us like that and allowed this to happen?"

She was about to defend herself again, but—in spite of the soft spot I've always had for Ma—I quickly cut her off. "I've got to tell you something important, Ma. Listen to me. We're all going on the Sally Jessy Raphael Show and we're going to tell the world what happened to us."

She didn't know what to make of this news. She fidgeted with her coffee mug, and her eyes were everywhere but on me.

"And I've got to tell you, Ma, that they're all lining up behind Dad. They're going to be on that show and they'll say all of this happened because of you."

"No, no," she said, shaking her head, "That's not true, that's not how it was."

"I'm going to stick up for you, Ma, but I can only help you if you go on the show. That's the only way you're going to get out of this—"

"I can't go on TV," she said.

Then she said, "What about Carl?"

"I already asked him." I was lying. I hadn't so much as breathed a word about the show to him. I pressed ahead. "And I told him I was taking the paperwork with me as proof of what happened. He's already agreed and he's blaming this whole thing on you."

"I had no choice, you know that!" She was nearly screaming by now. "I did what he told me to, that's all."

"Well, that's not what he's telling us."

I wasn't concerned that my mother might learn the truth; she hadn't spoken to my father in years.

"If you're going to sit back and stay off the show, you know what's going to happen? We're all going to be there and he's going to make you look like the bad guy."

My gentle, mild-mannered mother was fuming. "I'm not going to allow that to happen," she said. "What do I do to get on the show? How do I get there?"

I had Ma where I wanted her. "We'll make all the arrangements, Ma," I said.

Now came the harder part. When I drove up to my father's place in Londonderry, my heart was beating very fast. When I told him we were going on the show, he said, "Listen, let's not talk here. Come on, let's just go down the block and get something to drink."

Well, I figured, if it was going to make him more relaxed, why not? So we went into this little lounge and I bought him a beer, hoping to loosen him up. I did the same thing I'd done with my mother. I pulled out the clips and said, "So what's this all about? How did this happen?"

His reaction couldn't have been more different from Ma's. He barely glanced at them; he knew what they said. Instead of defending himself he began to talk about my mother.

"Maybe you were too young to remember, but she ran off to Connecticut. She left all of you. She was a no-good slob. She ran off with that son of a bitch."

I knew who the "son of a bitch" was. My father was talking about Bob King, the man Ma had had an affair with before she met my father. The man who, like me, had light hair and hazel eyes.

"Oh yeah," he said, "I looked for her for weeks—she was in Connecticut, she was in New York, she was all over. I know I was bad, but I never pulled the kind of stuff she did—I never ran off like that. And she left you all alone and I was trying to do my best and take care of you kids. But I had to go to work, I had to keep a roof over our heads. So it was hard." He shook his head, muttering. "She'd just left you like that."

He was playing the same game he always did. In my father's world, things were always someone else's fault.

I reminded him again about the show, and then, after I'd given it some time to sink in, added that Ma had agreed to go on, too. He looked up from his beer and frowned.

"You know," I went on, "she's going to destroy you on that show."

"I don't care," he grumbled, "I don't care."

But I could see that he *did* care. I pressed him. "She's going to be up there, telling the whole world that you were the one who abused both us and her. And everyone's going to end up hating you. You'll have no friends, no family. You'll be all alone."

He still pretended it didn't matter to him. Then he made it seem like he was changing the subject. "I've got to get a horse," he said. "And I got to make some repairs on the house and put some money in the business. Got to get some new equipment."

I knew what he was doing. He wasn't changing the subject at all. He was trying to bargain with me, seeing whether he could get a little money out of this deal.

I saw this coming, and I'd come prepared. "I'll tell you what, Dad, I'm going to pay you to go on the show. I'll give you what you need for the horse."

My father never pulled any punches. "Well, I could use about six hundred dollars."

I had brought a lot of cash with me for this very reason. I pulled out my wallet and counted out six crisp one-hundred-dollar bills. "There you are, six hundred bucks."

I wanted him to take the money. For as rotten as my father could be, money talked in his world, and I knew this—with the money in hand, he'd feel obligated. His word might not mean anything, but money did; money was better than his word, and it was certainly better than a guilt trip. I told him that the show would also pay him for going on, so he'd make more than a thousand dollars.

After we sealed the deal, I said, "Think about it, Dad, she's going on that show to make you look like the bad guy. She'll say you did things you probably didn't even do. The only way you can defend yourself is to go on, and we'll stick up for you. If you do that, then everybody's going to think she's the bad guy, not you."

He liked what he was hearing. "Yeah, yeah," he was saying. He could already picture himself up on the stage, I could tell. "I'll tell everything about her. She won't know what hit her." But then he had another thought. "I'm not getting on the same plane with her to go to New York."

"That's not how it's going to work. They'll fly you and Ma and us all separately. No one is together until we go on TV."

He nodded. "Okay, if that's how it is."

After that I thought we had him.

But just two days before we were supposed to go on the show, he backed out. I got a call from my brother Joseph. "He's not going," Joseph said.

I immediately got on the phone and called my father. There was no answer, but I knew he was there, so I got in the car and drove to his house. I was so mad, that I tore down the highway at eighty miles an hour. When I got there I didn't bother ringing the bell. I just opened the door and barged right in. He was sitting in the living room in the dark, nursing a beer.

"I've changed my mind," he said. "I'm not going, and there's nothing you can do to make me go. You can have your money back, if you want."

He wanted to give me my money back? This was going to be tough. Then I had an idea. Maybe I could get him on the show without his having to get on a plane to New York at all.

"Well, how about we do you via satellite? That way you don't have to go to New York. You'll be in a studio in Manchester and they'll beam you into the show by satellite."

He didn't know anything about satellite transmission, so he had no idea you could do something like this.

"You do that, Dad, you sit for an hour in a studio and you answer Sally's questions, and that's all you have to do." I looked at him, caught his eye, and held it for a long moment. I knew how hungry he was, and I needed to cut right to the heart of what was important to him. "And you can keep that money."

He looked back at me, and after the moment passed he gave one short nod.

The next day—a Tuesday—we flew in three separate groups to New York. The only one who didn't come with us was Joseph. He stayed behind to make sure my father got to the TV station in Manchester. We were put up in three hotels. It was a whole new experience for all of us, since hardly anyone had been to New York. The night before the show, my siblings and I got together at the Hard Rock Café. Everyone was in a celebratory mood, toasting me because I was the one responsible for arranging the whole thing. And having some extra cash in their pockets for their appearance only made them more excited. They were sure that by tomorrow they'd all be stars. I knew they thought there would be a payday coming soon, and I didn't want to say anything to puncture their dreams. Let them think what they wanted. I was there on a totally different mission. But I don't think any of us, whatever our motives, had any idea what we were really getting ourselves into.

Early the next morning limos were waiting in front of our hotels to take us to the studio. I couldn't believe how well things were going. Everything was falling into place. But I should have figured there would be a hitch. When I walked into the studio, Sally's producer came up to me and said, "I just talked to your brother Joseph in New Hampshire. He said when he went to pick up your father this morning your father told him he wasn't going to do it. So I guess that we'll have to do the show without him."

Suddenly I felt like a hamster, treading a wheel.

But I had no intention of letting him slip away. I was determined to get him on the show, no matter what it took. We had only forty minutes before we were to go on the air. Everybody else was already there, including my mother.

I got him on the phone. I said, "I'm here in New York, in the producer's office, and they tell me you're not going to the studio."

"That's right," he said. "There's nothing you can do to make me change my mind."

"Listen, I'm going to tell you some things I didn't tell you before. What Ma is going to say about you on the TV show isn't only going to make it impossible for you to walk out in public, but you stand a very good chance of going to jail."

"What?"

"I've got a piece of paper here," I said. "And it says that the statute of limitations is still honored for five of your youngest kids. You've beaten those kids, and if they want to put you behind bars, they can do it. You're looking at twenty years per count, and you've got five counts here. Just to get you out on bail is going to cost you ten-thousand dollars. You'll spend the rest of your life in jail. Those kids are going to the DA when we get back home, and you're going to jail, and you can count on it. And this videotape we're going to make right now is going to be proof of what happened to us."

He was quiet for a moment, trying to work out in his mind the implications of what I'd just told him.

"Look," I said, "I think you should go on the show and defend yourself. It's your only way out of this. If you go on, I promise no one is going to press any charges."

I had him cornered, and he knew it. Finally he agreed.

But to make sure he didn't back out again, I said, "And remember the five kids here. I've got them standing right here. Would you like to talk to them? Do you want to hear it directly from them?"

He said no. In truth, I didn't think it likely any charges could be brought against him. I didn't have any piece of paper; I didn't have anything but the desire to make things right again. I was just making it up. I just didn't want to let him escape one more time. I wanted to give my brothers and sisters the chance all of us had been waiting for our entire lives, even without knowing it. And in some strange way, we'd be doing our parents a favor, too. They'd have a chance to explain why they'd done what they had to us. And if they couldn't explain or justify their actions—how could they?—maybe they'd have to acknowledge what they'd done, or just think about it in a way they hadn't before. Even that would be a victory. I wondered what they would say.

The first thing I was aware of when I walked out onto the set were the bright lights. They kept the room uncomfortably hot, and they looked like fireballs up in the ceiling. Then I noticed rows of empty seats. It wouldn't be long before they'd fill up with strangers. Technicians were running through the room, setting up multiple cameras and giving everyone microphones. I stopped dead for a second, thinking: *It's all happening; we're actually going to be on the air soon.* But I still couldn't quite grasp it. The concept of "live before a studio audience" still felt pretty alien to me.

The producers were all women. They were all pretty sharp-looking, and they were surprisingly friendly. College-educated, I thought. Career women, nice people, who greeted us with "Hi, honey," and "How are you doing today?" It was overwhelming for me, and probably for my brothers and sisters; they weren't used to being treated politely by such well-dressed people. It was like being on a different planet.

The producers gave us instructions, explaining where we were to sit. When I sat down, I looked around and spotted each of the cameras. The place was littered with them. I felt self-conscious, but also strong—a strange mix. I knew we were doing the right thing.

To be sitting on that stage and seeing my brothers and sisters all around me was incredibly moving. I'd initiated this because of them, and when I looked around I saw them—as always—as weak, hurt, damaged, and in need of help. For a long moment, the emotion—my love for them—flooded through me. I believed that by getting everyone to this show, I was helping to free us all from the hold our father had on us.

As for me, I looked forward to being able to keep the promise I'd made to that child in the mirror—to survive, grow up, and tell my father's big, dirty secret. The time had finally come to fulfill my mission.

Ma was seated to the right of the stage, and we sat on benches in the center. I looked out over the empty rows of seats, and wondered what adventures lay in store for us. We were going to be revealing our deepest, darkest family secret, and not just to a few other people but to *millions* of them. How would people—the public, strangers—react to our story? Would they listen? Would they be interested? Or would they point and laugh?

On the opposite side of the stage there was a big screen. That was where my father, after all my convincing, would appear, beamed live by satellite from Manchester. I turned my attention to the blank screen. No matter what maneuvering I'd done with my parents, the spotlight would be on *him* today, not her. He was finally going to be held accountable for his behavior. How would he react? Would he admit to any wrongdoing? Would he feel ashamed? Would he—I couldn't even bear to think about it—show any *regret? Apologize?*

Suddenly they opened some side doors and the audience started filing in. They looked like happy people—I caught at least a few smiles. Would they be prepared to listen to our horrible life story? Pretty soon, all the seats were filled. I was conscious of the stage lights, but was now also conscious of the pounding that had begun in my chest. A production assistant mouthed a near-silent countdown, and we were on the air. The screen came alive, and there was my father, looking gray and worn, a shadow of the man who'd once terrorized us. He had a pinched, nervous look on his face. My mother had put on the blank expression she usually wore when she was nervous. I thought that any minute she might start humming, the way she always did when there was trouble around the corner. But she stayed quiet.

Sally led off with a brief introduction—just our first names and our ages, careful not to say what town we were from. After that, she told the audience that we'd all been abused by our father and abandoned by both our parents as kids. Out of the corner of my eye, I noticed some members of the audience fidget a little in their seats. *Hang in there,* I told them silently. *There's more.*

Then she asked us—one by one—to describe our childhoods. It was tough on everybody to get the words out, but once the words started coming it was even harder to stop.

My older sister, Susan, opened up in a way I'd never heard before. All the pent-up rage at the mistreatment she'd endured just exploded. I think even she was surprised at how angry she was. Tears were spilling down her cheeks. She demanded to know what my father was thinking when he dragged her around by the hair. She showed us—and the audience—the bald spots she still had. She was shouting and crying at the same time, but making herself perfectly clear. She had the audience's complete and undivided attention. She had ours, too.

Then it was John's turn. He talked about the beatings he'd taken over the years—how our father had beaten him for trying to protect Ma, how he made us betray each other, and then beat us the very next day. Tears began to roll down his face, too.

One by one, our stories came pouring out. Most of them were directed at the man on the screen:

I feel hatred for you.

You beat me because I didn't vacuum the rug.

You used to punch me each and every day.

You used to beat my mother up in the closet. I tried to stop you because I loved her.

You used to smash our faces in our dirty diapers.

You pulled me over your head and dropped me on the cement floor on my back. I have chips in my spine to this day. They said I was unconscious.

I watched my brother get beat, and I cried and begged you to stop. You told me I'd be next if I didn't shut my mouth.

When we were done, there was a long silence. Sally waited for a second to let it all sink in, and to let us dry our eyes and blow our noses. Then she did what she is so good at: She confronted my father. She strode up to the screen and asked whether what my brothers and sisters were saying was true. "You've heard what they're saying. Are they lying to me?"

A small hesitation. And then he replied—just one word.

"No."

"They aren't lying to me?"

"They're not lying." His voice was barely audible and he was looking away from the camera.

"How could this happen?" Sally demanded.

"It happened," he said. His head was moving slightly, like he had a tic I'd never noticed before.

I almost fell out of my chair when he said that. I didn't think he'd admit to any of it.

"But how?"

"I had stress. I had bad luck. I was so stressed-out half the time, workin' all my life to bring up these kids." He paused. "So maybe I could have done better."

Everything about that confession sounded wrong. "Workin' all my life to bring up these kids." You fed us *pig bread!* I felt like shouting. "So maybe I could have done better." It was ludicrous. It was as if he'd just gotten out of line on a few isolated occasions.

"Did you hate Wayne?" Sally asked him, using me as an example, because she'd met with me, and knew me better than she knew the others.

"No," he said.

"Did you think you were guilty of anything?" Sally pressed him.

"I don't know," he said, showing that tic again.

But when we made specific accusations, he denied them one by one. Raise Michael in the air and bang him down like a rag doll? "No, I never did that." Pull Susan's hair and drag her down the hallway? "No, not me, Ma'am."

He was swerving from a great height, like a badly balanced crane. He admitted the whole thing, and then denied pieces of it.

I think he was ashamed—maybe he was in denial, too. You could see how he flinched whenever these issues were raised. He might have been abusing us without realizing that what he was doing *was* abuse. I wondered if that was possible. And being charged with these abuses before a live audience was having a real effect on him. I'm sure he regretted coming on the show, but I'd given him little choice. And once he was there, he had nowhere to run.

All this time my mother was sitting there as if she had nothing to do with us. Naturally she was ready with her excuses when Sally asked her how she could have allowed Carl to beat up her kids. What was she doing? Wouldn't any mother protect her kids from harm, no matter what? Even if it meant fighting back or leaving the abusive husband?

My mother looked surprised. She said there was nothing she could do. She was helpless. Carl was in complete control over her, and over everyone. She acted as if she were as much a victim as her children. To prove her point, she said that, on their wedding night, Carl had beaten her within an inch of her life and knocked her unconscious. That really got to the audience, especially the women. They seemed outraged but also baffled. One woman stood up and asked my mother, "How come you didn't leave your husband once he did that? Why did you stay married to him?" All the women in the audience agreed that, if their husbands had done that to them on their wedding night, they'd have walked out on them and never come back.

People have always thought Ma seemed a bit slow mentally. Whether she is or not, I don't think Ma got it. It wasn't the way she looked at the world.

I think she expected her children to rally to her side, but that wasn't happening. Eventually Susan and John and Michael—the older kids— began to ask her why she'd run off and abandoned them. Why hadn't she left them with enough food? My mother was blindsided; she looked dazed, like she couldn't figure out what had hit her. She stammered more excuses, but I think it was clear to the audience that she wasn't the innocent victim she'd claimed to be. She still refused to accept any responsibility. By this point, my brothers and sisters were coming around to my view, that she was probably just as guilty as our father, even though she was helpless to defend herself to some extent.

I take pride in being a strong man. I've cried before, sure—when I got beat up as a kid, the day my son died, sitting in the truck the day I saw my school picture. But those times, I was either little or there was no one around to see me. But when Sally got to me and explained to the audience that I was the one who'd arranged for the family to go on the show, I began to lose my grip on my emotions.

My whole life lay before me—live before a studio audience. Observant—even in these strange moments in the spotlight—I was trying to gauge the audience members' reactions. Judging from the gasps and groans that followed some of our comments, they seemed sympathetic. But did they pity us? Worse, were we coming across as that freak show? I didn't think so, and I certainly hoped not.

As for my father, I realized that an important—and maybe inevitable—reversal had occurred. All our lives it had been my father against us. He had the power and we were at his mercy. Now, in front of millions of people, we had turned the tables. *We* had the power, and he couldn't even look the camera in the lens. That did it. I started to cry.

As with our confessions, once the crying started, it was hard to stop. I cried out of sadness, I cried out of pain, I cried out of relief, and I cried because of a release that had been a whole lifetime in coming.

There was something else, too, that came out with my tears. There was a decision. At that moment, I decided I didn't have any parents. They'd ceased to be parents the moment my father had taken his fist to us and my mother had stood by and watched. The person who was supposed to be my father was an imposter.

As always with me, I mourned more for my brothers and sisters than I did for myself. I knew I could handle this final break through the barriers of denial, but I worried about them. They'd been in denial to a greater degree than I had, and my older siblings had been in denial longer. When you come out of denial, it feels like you're walking from a black cave into harsh sunlight. The light pierces your body all over. It pours stinging into your eyes until you have to shut them. It hurts.

Between tears, I looked around, sadly. We formed a row of orphans—crying, grown-up orphans—damaged and unloved.

At the same time, I was proud, knowing I'd finally confronted him, and now it had come time to be free of the fear. It was all those things at once—being so overwhelmed with sadness and happiness and pain, and yet at the same time feeling so much closer to being whole. I had the satisfaction of knowing that I could look that child I had been in the eyes and say, I've done this for both of us. I kept the promise I made to you.

Sally threw her arms around me and gave me a hug. It was a caring, motherly gesture that reminded me of when I was in Mrs. Cole's class on the first day of school, learning to read and write. But I didn't have time to dwell on this. Sally wanted to know whether I felt angry. I thought about her question, and decided no, I wasn't angry—but I was enormously, tremendously sad. I denounced my father, and I told Sally, my family, the audience, and my father that I did so: I had no father. But the person who played the role of my father—the man on the live feed into the studio—was a man I did not hate. I said all this, and as I said it I was looking up at the screen, straight at him. He wasn't looking at me, though; he was just staring straight ahead, with no emotion on his face.

It was true. I didn't hate my father. If I had, I'd have been submitting to a negative power, and I'd made a conscious choice to live positively a long time ago. To do so is healthier; it lessens your hatred, and decreases the "what-ifs"—which are meaningless, anyway, because you can't turn back the clock.

So no, I didn't hate him. What I felt for him was—first, pity, and second, rejection of him as my father. That second feeling made it possible for me to feel the first: I could hate him when I still regarded him as my father. And when I didn't, I felt sadness for my life and for him.

I felt especially sad for my brothers and sisters, because they were where I used to be, just coming out of their denial. I knew what the road ahead would be like for them—long and bumpy. But they'd get through.

Finally, at the end of the show I felt an overwhelming sense of gratitude—I was glad we'd done it, and I was glad it was over. It was exactly what we'd needed, our day in court—not in a court of law, but of public opinion—and, finally, other people—the outside world—understood. Still, way too much had been lost to ever make up in an hour or two on TV.

Even though we hadn't each gone on the show with the same agendas, we'd all ended up getting something huge out of it. I don't think anyone expected anything this big; I certainly didn't. That we were revealing to the world what had gone on was important, but, more than that, we were revealing it to each other for the first time. Now we had validation. It wasn't just us anymore. By putting it into words on TV, we were making it real in a way that it had never been for any of us. When Sally asked my father, "How could this happen?" those words meant everything. That was the question we'd all been carrying around with us our whole lives. And the way she said it—as if she was acknowledging how hard it was even for her to believe that a father could have done what he had to his children. *How could this happen?*

His answer couldn't have been simpler, or less helpful.

"It happened."

After the show, the impact of having confronted our father and broken the silence made me feel like I'd passed some kind of strange coming-of-age ritual. But then life took another one of its surprising turns, and things got worse before they got better.

The problem had a lot to do with our expectations—my brothers' and sisters' and mine—about the show. As I've said, for me the show was about helping them—and myself—to heal, and doing it by getting everything out there in the open, and confronting our parents about it. Some of my siblings wanted the same thing; others wanted fame and wealth. But all in all, I don't think any of us were prepared for the pain we'd have to go through to get all the way there.

The show had been successful for helping my brothers and sisters come out of denial about the way we grew up. But now that they realized they were wounded, they didn't know how to control the bleeding.

Instead, they turned on me. "We should never have gone on that show," they said. "All you wanted was to drag us through the mud. How could you do that?"

"My father won't talk to me," one of my brothers complained. "My mother won't talk to me. At least I had parents. Now I have nothing." Most of my other brothers and sisters said they felt the same way.

They had to have been in touch with our father. The words they were using could have come right out of his mouth: "How could you go on that show and humiliate him? How could you do that to him? After he raised you. . ."

Then they began to say, "We shouldn't have listened to you. We shouldn't have done that to him."

It got worse; it turned personal. "Sally paid you big bucks, didn't she? Paid you to do this to him. She paid you to ruin him."

This wasn't true.

"You're a nutcase. Why don't you go to a shrink?"

And the worst, from a very angry brother: "Dad's going to get you. He's going to catch you in your yard and blow you away with a shotgun."

Well, he didn't come after me with a shotgun, but things were getting so bad, it almost would have been better if he had. At least it might have cleared the air and stopped the incessant badgering and attacks. The phone rang off the hook at all hours of the day, seven days a week. I was fighting with my brothers and sisters, screaming at them on the phone. I felt unappreciated, and I couldn't control my anger. It was overwhelming.

I had always had that little voice in my head that said, *You're no good. You're dysfunctional, a lowlife, a loser.* And I'd learned to counteract it most of the time, to shift my attention or talk myself out of it. But since we'd been on the show, the voice had gotten even more insistent. I was hearing it constantly, and I couldn't make it stop. On top of that, I was angry all the time, and I couldn't keep a lid on it. I kept getting into fights and stupid arguments—anything could set me off. And I was totally confused. This was not supposed to happen. Things should have been better after we went on that show.

On the show, I'd concluded, *That's it, then. They weren't parents to us. We never had parents. And I can distance myself from them.* Like it was a magic answer. But there's little magic in this world that you don't put there yourself, and that conclusion was not the answer.

Meanwhile, Sharon was having a really hard time. She was tired of the phone calls, and she was tired of my depression. My second marriage—which had started out with so much caring and love—was starting to look a little like my first. The two of us fought night and day. I said horrible things to her, like the things my father had said to my mother and sisters. It devastated me to hear that poison coming out of my mouth, but I was unhappy with myself and my life was spinning out of control.

One day when I came into the house I heard Sharon talking about me to her mother in the kitchen. I heard her mother say, "You should leave him. You'll be better off."

I walked into the kitchen, livid. "Get the hell out of my house and don't come back," I told Sharon's mother.

When she was gone, Sharon and I had a big, thundering, blowout argument. Sharon said she couldn't take my behavior anymore. If the calls from my family didn't stop, she was leaving. If I didn't take steps to reduce my anger, she was leaving. I left her with her ultimatum, and stormed out of the house.

It felt like everything was over. The whole world was against me. My son had died, and my first marriage had failed. The business I'd worked so hard to build was gone. Our beautiful dream house—gone. I'd disowned my parents. My brothers and sisters hated me. Now the woman I loved was about to leave me. If Sharon left, she'd take my beautiful daughters with her, and I'd lose them, too.

The positive side of me just melted away and left no trace. I crumbled, the hope totally gone—dust to dust.

I got into my truck and drove to our old house—my dream house—and pulled into the garage. The house hadn't been sold yet, so it was empty. The neighbors weren't around; I knew nobody would notice and try to stop me. The voice in my head kept repeating the same gloomy words. I was a failure, a loser, a fake. I didn't deserve anything good—not a gorgeous house, not a loving family, not even this truck I'd spent two weeks picking out. I was unworthy. I didn't deserve to live. Or if I did, I was too tired and beaten down. My fighting energy was down to almost nothing.

The garage door was shut. I sat in the cab of my truck, turned the ignition on, and rolled down the windows. It wouldn't take long, and it would be painless.

I looked at the clock on the dashboard—3:48 in the afternoon. I watched it go to 3:55, and then four o'clock. I breathed very deeply. My body was feeling very relaxed. I didn't smell anything.

Then I started thinking. I saw Sharon's face and the faces of my little girls—Amy, Tiffany, Emily—my treasures, all three. What kind of life would they have knowing their father had killed himself? *What will they think of me? Better yet, what do I want them to think of me?*

I wanted them to be proud of me, to point at me and brag about my coaching abilities, my successful business, or even just how I'd fought my way through hard times. I wanted them to talk about me with pride, not shame. And when it comes to suicide, there's mostly shame.

And I thought, *If I kill myself, everything my father ever said about me will be true. If I kill myself, he wins. If I kill myself the abuse wins.*

I'd been listening to a subconscious voice telling me to take the easy route away from the pain. *Go get drunk, smoke a joint, pop a pill—maybe this pain will go away for a few hours.* Worse—*Go pound somebody's head in—maybe you'll forget about the pain for a few minutes.* But the other side—the positive one, was struggling back.

Life has a way of bubbling up like a brook from under the heaviest of boulders. The part of me that kept me on track—the practical, positive side—hadn't been functioning. It was as if I'd been away from myself, and now I was back.

Suddenly I realized my wife and children loved me. I realized how much energy I still had, and how much I still wanted to do. In a flash, I realized just what I'd accomplished by simply surviving the giant, looping roller coaster of my life. I'd invested a lot in myself, and this, what I was going through, was a slump—a big one, but not something I couldn't pull through.

Our appearance on the Sally Jessy Raphael Show had forced my whole family to confront the truth, but none of us—least of all, and most surprisingly, me—were able to really deal with it. But suddenly, I got my nerve back. I guess the inner strength that had saved me when I was six years old and my father tried to kill me was still there. And once again, it saved me.

I turned off the engine and drove home. When I got home, I opened the door of the truck, got out, and went into the house. By the time I walked down the hallway to where Sharon was, I'd gathered up enough energy to give her at least a little of the comfort she must have needed.

Sharon was sitting on the couch in the living room crying. When I walked in, she glanced up, and then lowered her head again and continued to sob. I knew exactly what to do. I went right over to her and bent down on one knee. I took both of her hands in one of mine, looked into her face, and with the other hand wiped away some of her tears.

Watching her sadness, I felt tenderness for her all over again. I couldn't believe I'd actually been ready to give up the fight. I couldn't even remember why I'd been so mad at her. I could never stay mad at Sharon, anyway—she was way too vulnerable. After all these years, Sharon still needed me, and—miraculously—she still loved me. Those were two good reasons to live.

"Sharon," I said. She didn't want to look me in the eye. "Sharon," I said again, softly, steadying my gaze on her downcast eyes. "I'm sorry. I'm so sorry. Please, please forgive me." I said it one more time. "Please forgive me."

I promised her I would change. I'd get professional help or whatever it took to get this poison out of me. If I didn't keep my word, I told her, she should divorce me, the marriage would be over.

I looked at her and waited. Sharon sniffled and met my gaze. She asked me one question.

"Are you sure? Because I can't take this any more."

I nodded my head and made the promise.

It was a new beginning.

It took a month for me to admit to Sharon that I'd tried to commit suicide that day in the garage. I told her quietly as we lay facing each other on our bed after the girls had gone to sleep. Sharon wasn't exactly shocked, but I could see the concern—and the relief—in her face, still so pretty after all these years. By then, we both knew life was on another of its upward swings, and everything—for the moment—was good and safe.

When you come close to death, and then survive, the life you lead afterward is like a gift. The next few months were like that for Sharon and me; we were discovering each other all over again, holding hands sometimes and giggling like kids. Through talking with Sharon and really, really *listening* to her, I learned things about myself I didn't know—like how I sometimes, without knowing it, still took comfort in going back to the old ways of thinking that I was worthless. I called this kind of thinking "the poison," and that's exactly the effect it had on me—a gradual killing of my mind and spirit. It's like when I got off drugs. I try my best to detoxify.

Living *is* a gift, and part of accepting the gift is meeting the daily challenges the world throws your way. If one of those challenges makes me backslide—to back up for a few seconds or days and let the poison in—I try to have a little patience with myself. The important thing is not to punish yourself for backsliding, but just to keep moving forward, one day at a time.

The suicide attempt was a few years ago, and it feels very far away, now that life is good. I'm back on good terms with most of my brothers and sisters, some of whom have gone through abuse survival counseling. One of my sisters actually works for me now. She really enjoys it, and it brings us closer. Eventually, I got myself out of bankruptcy and rebuilt my business; it's making money again, and we do pretty well. I adjusted to the idea that losing my dream house didn't mean I couldn't have new dreams. My family and I now live in another beautiful house—not a mansion, but big enough, and warm, and comfortable.

I look around, and I don't believe a word of what I see in advertisements and on television—that change can happen overnight. Change is slow, and it takes willingness and a lot of hard work. The great thing is, if you put in the hours, in the end you get to look back and be amazed by how far you've come.

From time to time, I pull out something I keep in the bottom drawer of my desk. It's my school picture, the one I found in the government file—a normal-looking six-year-old boy with a chipped tooth and a too-short crewcut—my one visual link to the past. I look into the picture and remind myself that when I was that six-year-old boy, my father almost killed me for wetting my bed. What protected me then was finding the place in myself where I could take shelter from him, where I could hide and be safe—that inner strength we all have, someplace deep inside.

When I look at the picture, I experience different feelings. I feel connected to the child I saw in the mirror so many years before, as if I'm paying my respects to my past. I also feel proud that I kept my promise to him and, by living an improved life, that I continue to keep that promise. I feel stronger than that child was, but I also feel like he—the one who found the safe place—had always had the potential to be strong.

On a recent morning, I pulled out the picture again and studied it. I saw something I'd never noticed. A burst of light—probably the blinding fluorescent light the photographer brought with him—hits my forehead at an angle. There's a kind of gleam in my eye. The child in the photo is smiling, and at that moment he's not sad or scared. He's looking right into the camera, piercing the lens with his gaze. He doesn't look anxious, or depressed, or worried. He looks peaceful, almost content.

He's all right, I think.

And now the man in the mirror—grown up and living the closest thing possible to a normal life—smiles, too. I've made it, and I'm all right.

EPILOGUE

When my daughters were younger, I made sure they had plenty of toys. Stuffed animals, dollhouses, computer games, laser tag—whatever they wanted, they pretty much got. I guess that was because my parents didn't give us any toys. Instead, we got neglect, isolation, abuse, starvation.

My father did teach me some valuable things—how to suffer and how to survive. Ma was mostly indifferent, which taught me yet another important lesson—how to fend for myself. Both of them, either because of something they did or something they didn't do, made me feel worthless, and although I know now that I'm *not* worthless, I fight that feeling almost every waking moment.

When you're abused, the pain you experience has little to do with the hit. It's the swing that's the worst part, even if there's no follow-through. It's watching that swing coming, knowing that the person wielding the fist, or the hammer, or the pot of boiling water, is also the hand that feeds you, cleans you, gives you clothes to wear, makes sure you go to school. Or the one who decides to do none of those things.

For most of us, the love of a parent for a child is very simple. It's basic, like breathing. Maybe you don't see it coming, but once they're born, these little ones fill your entire world. It's like being in love.

I've never laid a hand on my kids, never even so much as given them a spanking. I've always done my best to be there for my two older children, Becky and Jimmy. They're both good people, independent and smart. Becky and I have a close relationship that I cherish. She's married now and I have a beautiful granddaughter. My granddaughter and I are crazy about each other and I see her all the time. I stay in touch with Jimmy and I dream of having him by my side every day—the kind of father-son relationship I've always wanted. I'll never give up on that dream.

Sharon and I did a good job with the younger ones. They're really good kids, but they're like all kids: They're not perfect, and I have a temper just like anyone else. But my love for them doesn't allow violence. The thought of hitting or otherwise hurting any one of them makes me sick.

I'm deeply involved in their lives. Amy, the cocky high-school student, is now sixteen, and she's exactly like me; she's her father's daughter. Besides being cocky, she has a good business sense, and she's a real go-getter. At fifteen, she ran a summer horse camp, and together with the money she earns teaching and training horses, she makes the monthly payments on her first car.

Tiffany, at fourteen, is Miss Fashion Queen. She's really into looking correct all the time, not a brunette strand or a dark eyelash out of place. She's got a nice, even temperament. She's always eager to help, the only one who cleans the house without being asked, the one who's sweet enough not to mind if her boyfriend spends weekends helping me out around the farm.

Emily's my thirteen-year-old fish eater. We're the only ones in the family who eat seafood. From the time she was a little munchkin, I used to take her to a local seafood shop. We still go all the time, and we bond over fish and chips, which I can now eat every day, any time I want to. (You remember Herb's Fish Market, where my father got fish and chips to eat in the car, and threw me the skin? These days, they tell me I'm their best customer.) Afterward, Emily and I bond again over a softball mound. I've coached Emily the longest of all the girls, and she's a real champ.

And then there's little six-year-old Elizabeth. When my softball team rides in local parades, Elizabeth sits in the front seat of the truck with her daddy. She's just as beautiful as the others—a petite little girl with long brown hair—and she's advanced, too. She's actually a fifteen-year-old in the body of a six-year-old. She does gymnastics, plays the piano, loves to dance. She's the kind of kid who doesn't need to have a friend; she amuses herself. She's got this little pink radio she takes with her everywhere. She talks to it, talks to her dolls, talks to herself. Watching her reminds me of the time I spent in the woods as a child, talking to the trees—my own world of imaginary friends.

My chest doesn't feel hollow when I look at my daughters. Instead, it's full of pride and love and this enormous, amazing happiness. Their future is really and truly limitless. In a few years, the three oldest ones will graduate from high school. From there, they can go on to do pretty much anything—maybe an equestrian college, a good career, and, eventually, some little babies running around. It doesn't matter what they do. They've turned out all right, and knowing that makes me so happy, my smile could split my face.

I refer to myself as a "born-again"—a born-again Healed Guy.

But it's not over. I'm still healing, and I'm learning all the time. For example, denial is a mysterious thing. It's got a lot of layers, and when you strip one away, underneath you may find yet another. When you're brought up to tell yourself—and other people—a story that's a complete lie about who you are, then you start to believe it, and it becomes how *you* see the world, too. When you want the lie to end, it's really hard to know how many layers you have to peel off to get to that place where denial ends and the truth begins.

When I decided I didn't have parents, I was lost in one of those layers. I now know that denying they exist isn't a solution to my problems. Still, pushing them out of my life temporarily was an important step. It helped me deal with my sadness about who they are, and it also helped me realize that I had to be my own mother and father—a realization everyone faces sooner or later.

I see my father about four times a year. He lives a few hours away in another town in New England. He's an old man now, broken and divorced and probably pretty darn lonely. I don't really forgive him, but I don't hate him. I know what he did to me was a reaction to his own sad childhood. When I look at him, I sometimes feel sorry for him. But to hate him, I'd have to turn on a negative part of myself that I've worked hard to bury. That kind of thinking can eat away at you; it's a disease worse than cancer. This is the choice I've made. You might say not hating him is more for me than it is for him, but it works—in the past four or five years, I've managed to let a lot of the bad feelings go. I'd so much rather stay upbeat, stay positive.

Each of us has some hurdle we need to get over, some past injury or hurt we have to come to terms with in order to move on. A few years ago, I tried to kill myself. A few years ago, I felt like I'd never get over the way I was raised or get past my feelings of worthlessness. And now? If you ask me whether I've made peace with my childhood, I don't know that I can answer that. I don't know that anyone can ever really predict his own future or step back far enough from himself to say how healthy he is. But I do know that, as with everyone else, it's a day-by-day struggle. The sight of broken glass and the sound of a car driving on gravel still bother me, but my days are usually pleasant, sometimes glorious, and almost always upbeat, even when they're challenging.

And I love my life.

So if that means I'm winning, then I'll accept that.

SELECTED RESOURCES

To Report Child Abuse

Childhelp USA® National Child Abuse Hotline

Toll-Free Phone: 1-800-4-A-CHILD (1-800-422-4453)
Website: http://www.childhelpusa.org

The Childhelp USA® hotline operates twenty-four hours a day. All calls are confidential.

Or check your phone book under "Child Abuse." You can also contact your local United Way for information about services in your area.

Suicide Prevention Information

National Suicide Prevention Hotline

Toll-Freee Phone: 1-800-suicide (1-800-784-2433)
Available from all fifty states, twenty-four hours a day.

> If you are feeling suicidal right now, if you are thinking about harming yourself or others, pick up the phone and call 911 or your local police or fire department. *It is an emergency.* There is immediate help for you. Make the call and wait for help to arrive.

American Foundation for Suicide Prevention

120 Wall Street, 22nd Floor, New York, NY 10005
Toll-Free Phone: 1-888-333-AFSP (1-888-333-2377)
Phone: 1-212-363-3500
Website: http://www.afsp.org; *E-mail:* inquiry@afsp.org

Breaking the Cycle of Abuse

National Domestic Violence Hotline

Toll-Free Phone: 1-800-799-SAFE (1-800-733-7233)
TTY: 1-800-787-3224
Website: http://www.ndvh.org

Offers information to men and women who want to stop the abusive cycle.

Parent Help USA

3848 Campus Dr. Suite 101 & 106, Newport Beach, CA 92660
Phone: 1-949-251-9274; *Fax:* 1-949-574-2437
Website: http://www.parenthelpusa.org; *E-mail:* sally@parenthelpusa.org

Teaches parents how to discipline children without hitting or harming them.

Support for Child Abuse Survivors

Childhelp USA® National Child Abuse Hotline

Toll-Free Phone: 1-800-4-A-CHILD (1-800-422-4453)
Website: http://www.childhelpusa.org

Counselors provide referrals to local agencies and adult survivor groups throughout the United States and Canada for ongoing support.

isurvive.org

Website: http://www.isurvive.org

Provides an anonymous online discussion for abuse survivors.

Education and Information

American Humane

63 Inverness Drive East, Englewood, CO 80112
Toll-Free Phone: 1-866-242-1877; *Fax:* 1-303-792-5333
Website: http://www.americanhumane.org

Since 1877, American Humane has been committed to preventing abuse and educating the public about the rights of both children and animals.

Child Abuse Prevention Association

Website: http://www.childabuseprevention.org

Contains definitions and helpful information on what to do if you believe a child is being abused or neglected.

National Clearinghouse on Child Abuse and Neglect Information

Toll-Free Phone: 1-800-FYI-3366 (1-800-394-3366)
Website: http://www.calib.com/nccanch/; *E-mail:* nccanch@calib.com

The nation's largest database of child maltreatment and related child welfare resources.

Further Resources

For more information, visit our online Website: http://www.waynetheodore.com